Coast Guard Approved Courses

Operator of
Uninspected Passenger Vessel

Take up to Six Paying Passengers

Fourth Edition

Captain Bryan Smith • Captain Neil Smith

US Captain's Training
Traverse City, Michigan

for those aspiring captains

First published by US Captain's Training in the United States of America.

Requests to the Publisher for permission should be addressed to the Permissions Department, US Captain's Training, 8256 South Watkins Lane, Traverse City, MI 49684, (866) 293-9308, website
https://uscaptainstraining.com/captains-license-contact

To order books or for customer service please call (866) 293-9308.

Acknowledgements

This book is intended to closely follow an online course curriculum created by US Captain's Training. It contains information produced and obtained from U.S. Department of Homeland Security and the United States Coast Guard (USCG). This title is published by US Captain's Training and any presence of the USCG's initials, name, or logo does not express endorsement by the USCG.

Disclaimer

The information in this book is true and complete to the best of our knowledge. The authors and publisher disclaim any liability in connection with the use of this information.

ISBN: 978-1-54396-769-2

Printed in the United States of America by Bookbaby.com

Use the coupon code "OUPVTEXTBOOK" and receive a $50 discount on the US Captain's Training Online OUPV Course from USCaptainsTraining.com.

Operator of
Uninspected Passenger Vessel

Take up to Six Paying Passengers

Rules of the Road
International and Inland

.

Rules of the Road - International and Inland

The International Rules were formalized in the Convention on the International Regulations for Preventing Collisions at Sea, 1972, and became effective on July 15, 1977. The Rules (commonly called 72 COLREGS) are part of the Convention, and vessels flying the flags of states ratifying the treaty are bound to the Rules. The United States has ratified this treaty and all United States flag vessels must adhere to these Rules where applicable. President Gerald R. Ford proclaimed 72 COLREGS and the Congress adopted them as the International Navigational Rules Act of 1977.

These Rules are applicable on waters outside of established navigational lines of demarcation. The lines are called COLREGS Demarcation Lines and delineate those waters upon which mariners shall comply with the Inland and International Rules. On December 24, 1981, the Inland Navigational Rules Act of 1980 took effect on inland waters shoreward of the COLREGS Demarcation Line and on the Western Rivers. Two years later, the same rules also took effect on the Great Lakes. For the first time, a single set of navigation rules replaced three separate rules-of-the-road that existed for inland waters, the Great Lakes, and the Western Rivers. This represented a dramatic and welcome change; it also ended a century of confusing patchwork legislation and rulemaking.

Almost 90% of the inland rules are now the same as the international rules. Many candidates for "Inland" licenses are not tested on the COLREGS because these rules do not apply to "Inland" waters. However, since 1977, the line of demarcation between inland and international waters moved closer to shore. You will be in COLREGS waters if you travel through the "pass" or "inlet," run "outside along the beach," or operate in Maine waters north of Casco Bay, in Puget Sound, or in Alaskan waters. The boundary between inland and international waters is the COLREGS Line of Demarcation shown on many nautical charts and described in 33 CFR 80. There are two reasons why mariners study the navigation rules. The first and most obvious reason is that knowledge of the rules is necessary to prevent collisions between vessels. The second reason is that most professional mariners must study for various Coast Guard license exams and renewals that generally include a section on the navigation rules with a minimum passing grade of 90%.

How the Rules Are Organized

The navigation rules are built like a pyramid; to understand the rules, start at the top and work down. Consequently, we will begin your study on RULE 1 and follow through to RULE 37. Building a good, solid knowledge of the rules will take time; it cannot be done overnight.

The new inland navigational rules are based upon the 72 COLREGS that apply outside the "lines of demarcation" drawn on most coastal charts. Most of the rules are exactly (or very nearly) the same. Where they differ we will highlight the differences. Understanding the 72 COLREGS provides the basis for understanding the Inland Rules. In the "Navigation Rules" book the International Rules (COLREGS) are on the left-page and the Inland rules on the right-page.

The Vocabulary Used In the Rules

You must learn the vocabulary used in the rules. The main problem in dealing with the vocabulary will not be with "big words" you may never have seen before but rather how words and phrases, even simple ones, are used in the rules. Each word or phrase has a very definite and exact meaning that must be recognized from the moment it is introduced.

Words and phrases used in these rules must serve two purposes.

First, they must mean something to you because you must use them every working day. They must also carry that same meaning to all others governed by them.

Second, they must convey the same single, precise meaning in court when necessary to judge responsibility for a collision. Such collisions must be a result of a human or mechanical failure and not a failure of the navigation rules to clearly define responsibility.

You must try to understand these rules from both of these standpoints. However, from a practical aspect you must be able to identify and appropriately react to lights, shapes, whistle signals, and the responsibilities between vessels so that you can function on the job. You must also understand and apply the basic meaning of the rules so that you will have a leg to stand on if called upon to defend your actions in court. To obtain any license, you will not be able to settle for anything less than complete mastery of the rules.

You should make the new words you learn a part of your working vocabulary. Do not avoid using them because they are new, unfamiliar, or sound funny.

Reading the Rules

Whenever one rule refers to any other rule, or part of a rule, stop and look up the reference to see exactly what it says and how it fits in with the rule you are studying. Each reference is significant, you should track it down so you can understand the full meaning of the rule you are reading. This takes time, is a pain in the neck and is called "study"! This study will require your concentration, close attention to details, and probably more time than you expected to spend.

Mnemonic Rhymes List

- yellow over white hauser towing at night

- Yellow over yellow I'm a pushing fellow (also hip towing) *inland only*

- 2 in a row is a tug and a tow

- 3 in a row is a tug and a long tow (over 200 m) or a long tug and a short tow (head on)

- 4 in a row is a long tug and a long tow (head on)

- Red over green, I'm a sailing machine

- Thumbs down to sailboaters under sail <u>and</u> power

- Green over white, trawling at night

- Red over white, fishing at night

- Thumbs up to fisherman (nets, lines, trawls)

- Red over red, my captain is dead – N.U.C.

- Red white red, captain making bread – R.A.M.

- White over red, pilot ahead

- A flashing red and yellow is a public service fellow

- Flashing blue, hide your brew (police)

- Single or double all around white, anchored at night

- One or two white and two red, shallow water ahead (vessel aground)

Definitions

over	<u>O</u>ver Taken
night	<u>N</u>.U.C. - ex. Circ.
Rooms	<u>R</u>.A.M. - Work
For	<u>F</u>ishing - nets, lines, Trawls
Sale	<u>S</u>ailing - under Sail only
Plus	<u>P</u>ower - machinery
Supper	<u>S</u>ea Plane - Well Clear

Under Way

- not @ Anchor
- not Made Fast
- not Aground

making Way	not under Way
A ·——→ ·B	· A (drifting)

Sailing Vessel

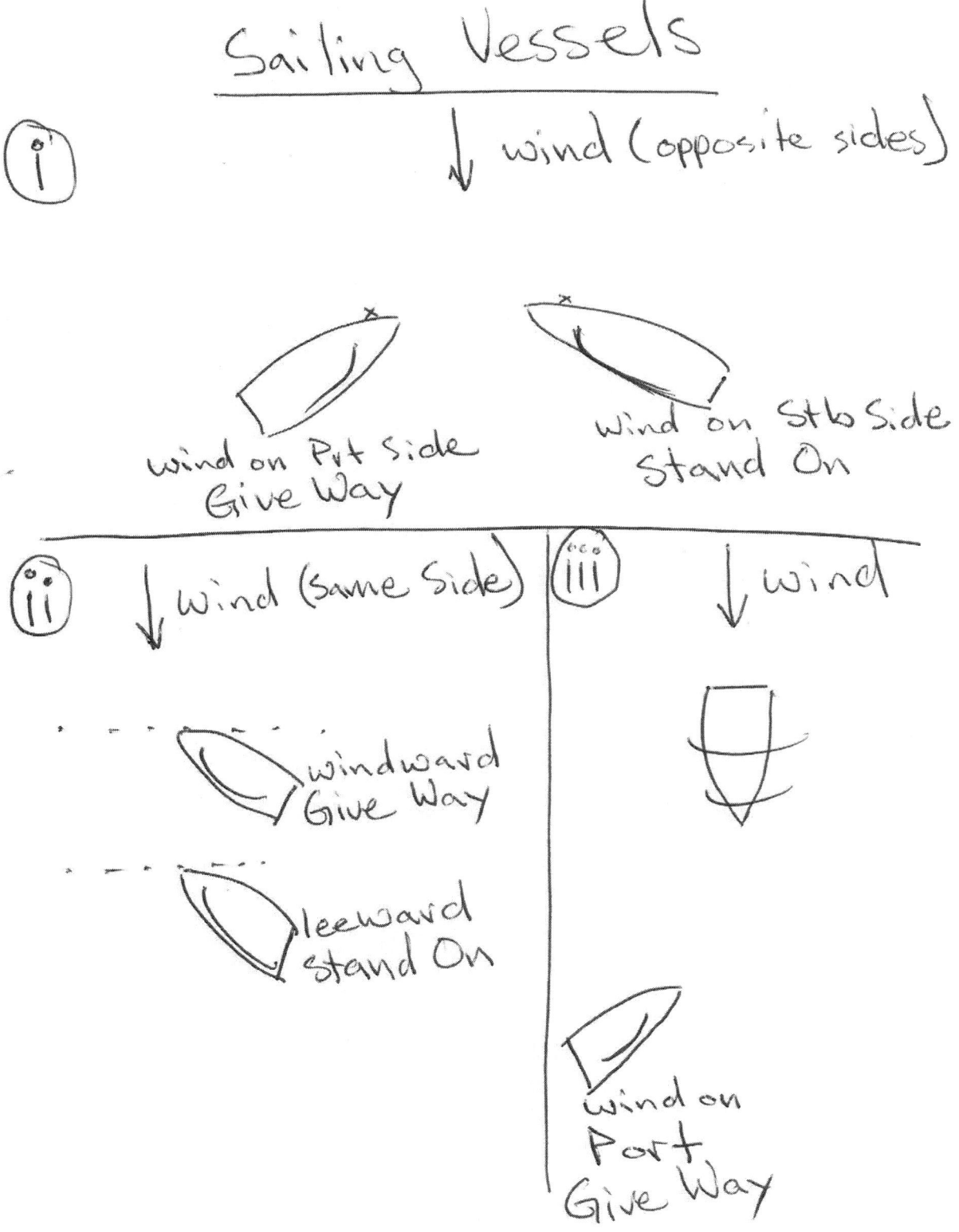

Sailing Vessels

(i) ↓ wind (opposite sides)

wind on Prt Side
Give Way

Wind on Stb Side
Stand On

(ii) ↓ Wind (Same Side)

windward
Give Way

leeward
Stand On

(iii) ↓ wind

wind on
Port
Give Way

Situations

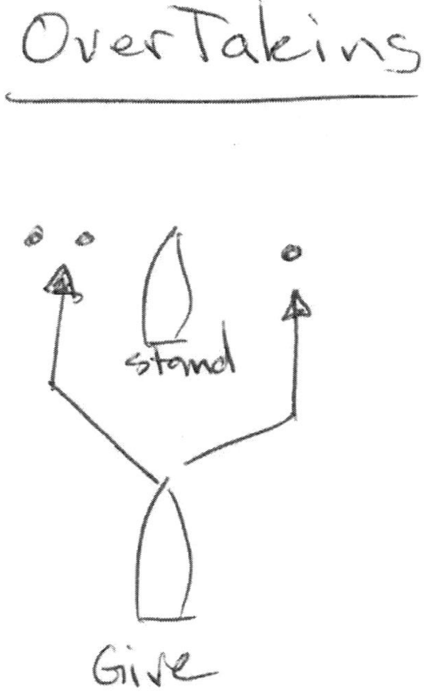

OverTaking

stand

Give

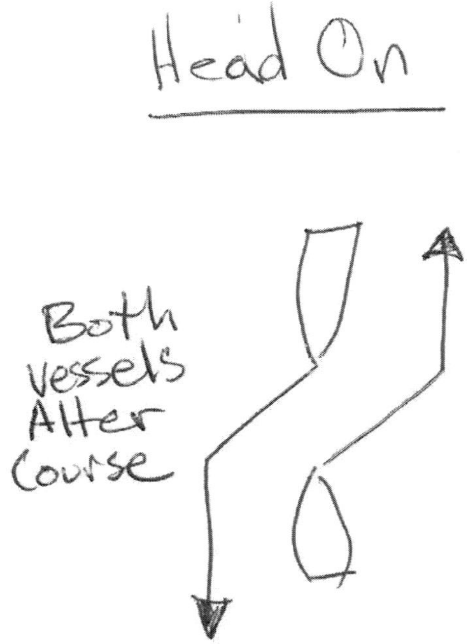

Head On

Both
vessels
Alter
course

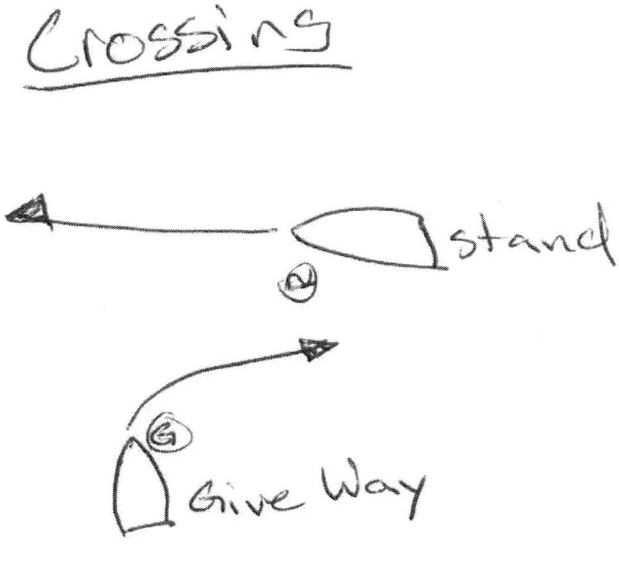

Crossing

Stand

Give Way

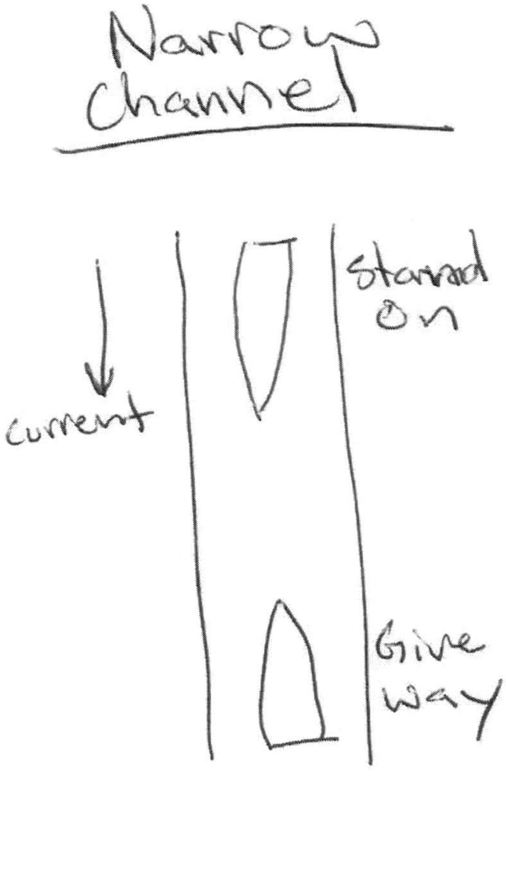

Narrow
Channel

current

Stand
On

Give
Way

Day Shapes

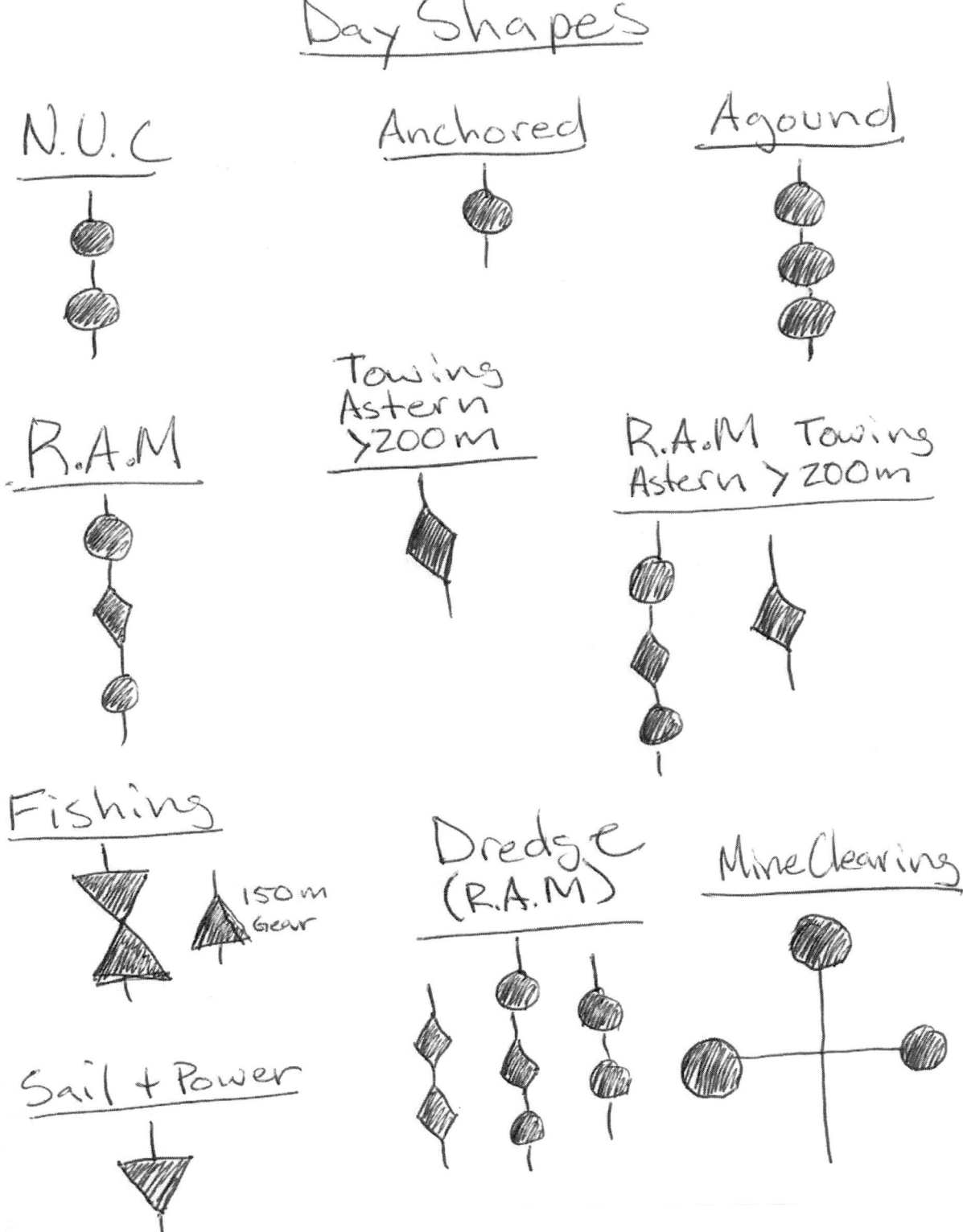

Light Definitions

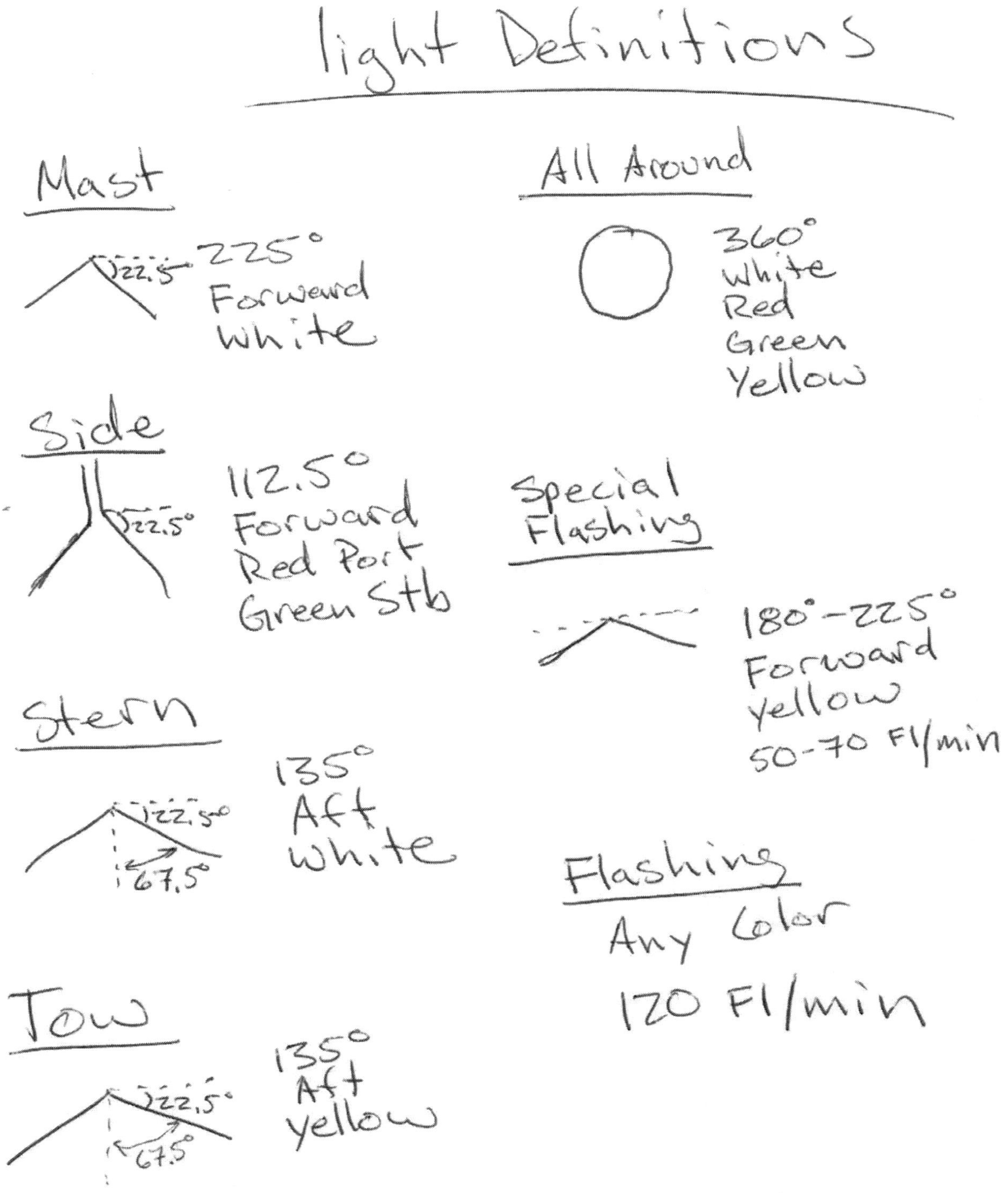

light Definitions

Mast

225°
Forward
White

Side

112.5°
Forward
Red Port
Green Stb

Stern

135°
Aft
White

Tow

135°
Aft
yellow

All Around

360°
White
Red
Green
Yellow

Special Flashing

180°-225°
Forward
Yellow
50-70 Fl/min

Flashing

Any Color

120 Fl/min

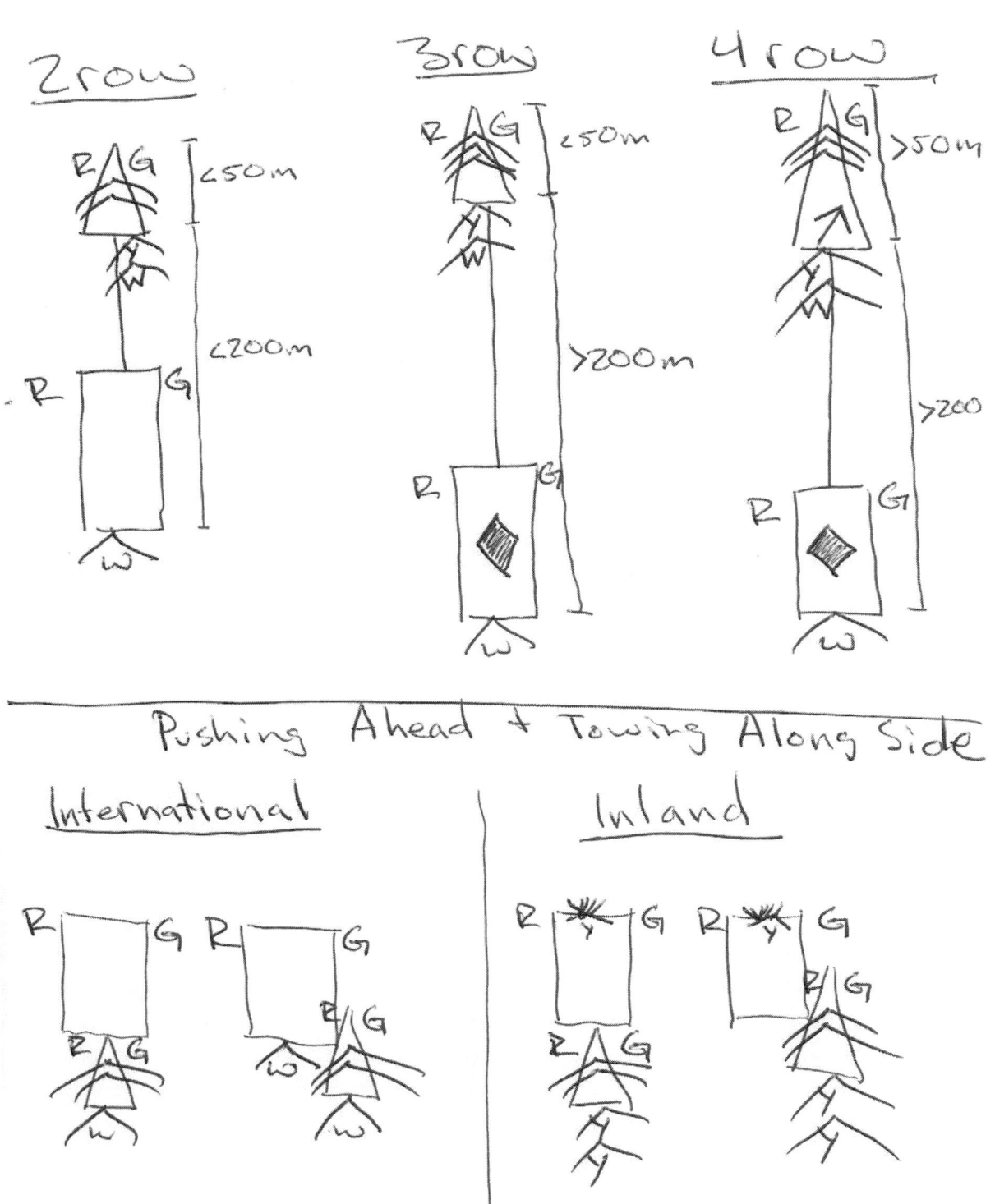

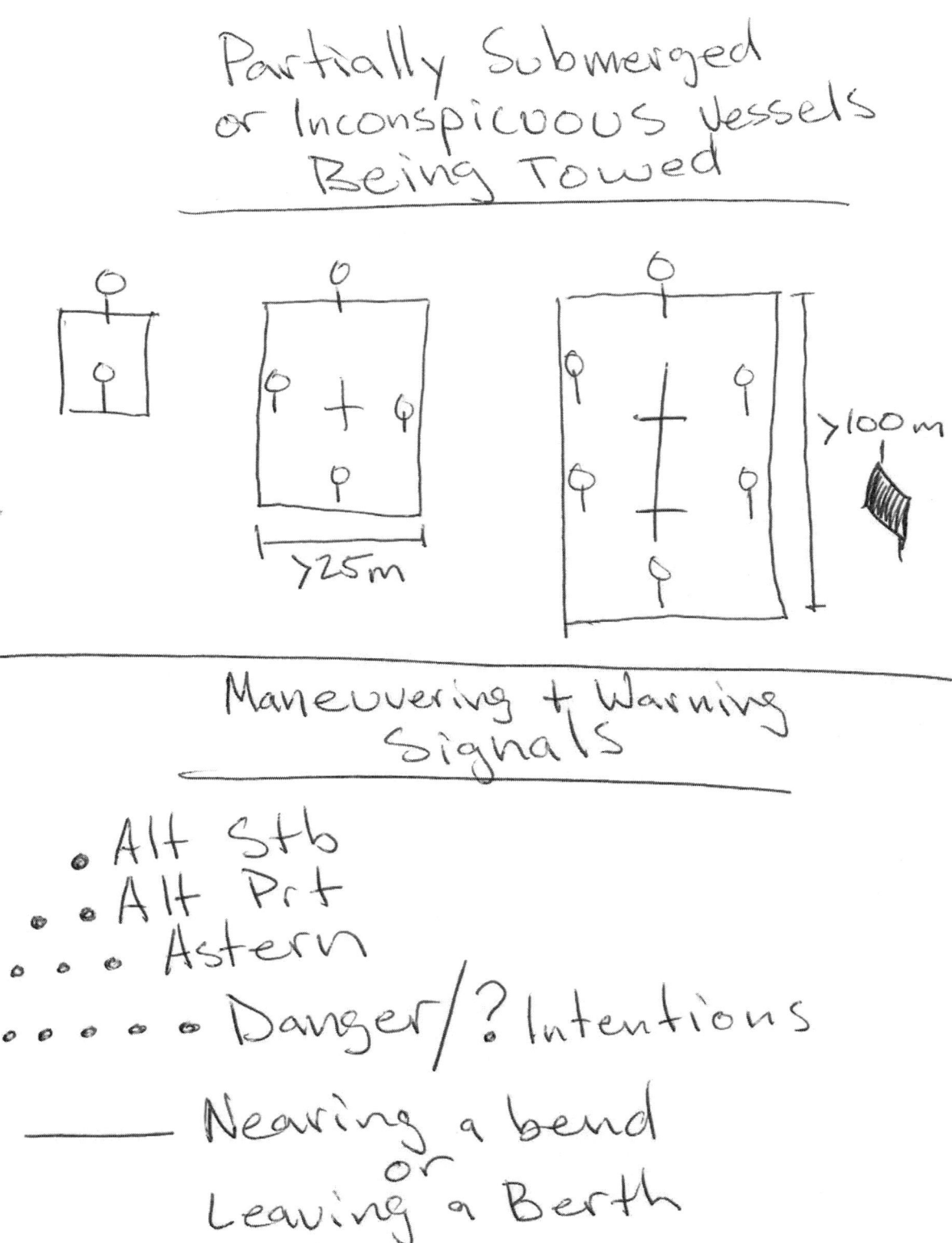

Partially Submerged or Inconspicuous Vessels Being Towed

>25m

>100m

Maneuvering + Warning Signals

- Alt Stb
- Alt Prt
- Astern
- Danger / ? Intentions

——— Nearing a bend
or
Leaving a Berth

Sound Signals

Whistle Signals of Vessels
Underway in Restricted Visibility
@ 2min

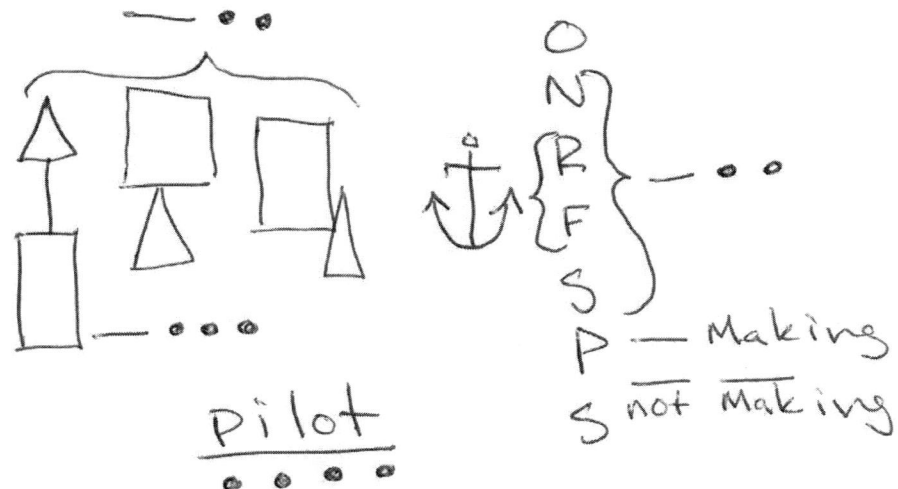

Pilot

— Making

not Making

Bells + Gongs of Vessels
Anchored and Aground @ 1 min

Anchored (shall)	Aground (shall)
<100m ⌇⌇⌇⌇	<100m lll ⌇⌇⌇ lll
>100m ⌇⌇⌇ ♪♪♪♪	>100m lll ⌇⌇⌇ lll ♪♪♪♪

MAY
(whistle)

DIAGRAM 1   DIAGRAM 2   DIAGRAM 3

DIAGRAM 5   DIAGRAM 6   DIAGRAM 7   DIAGRAM 10

DIAGRAM 11   DIAGRAM 12   DIAGRAM 14

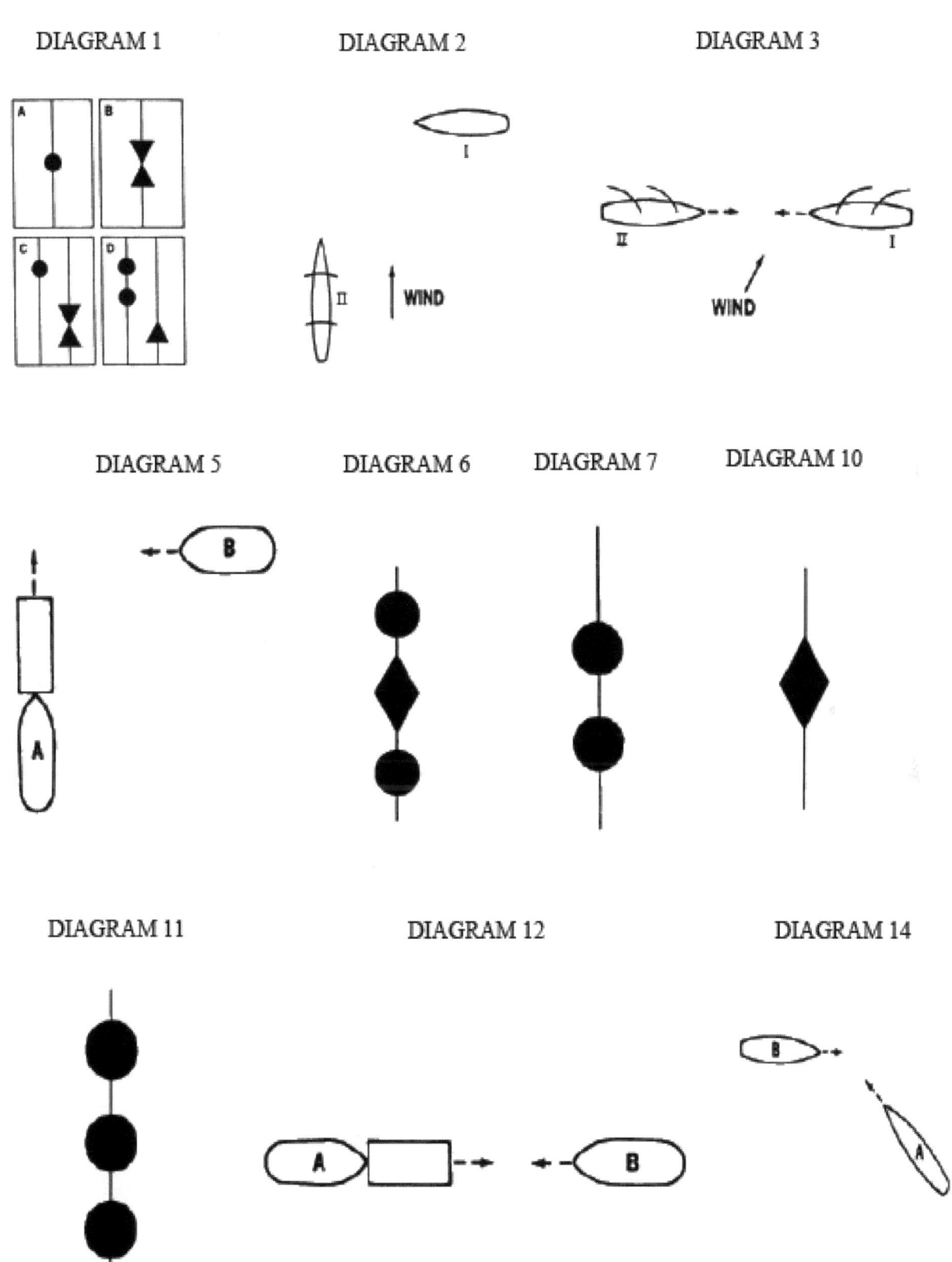

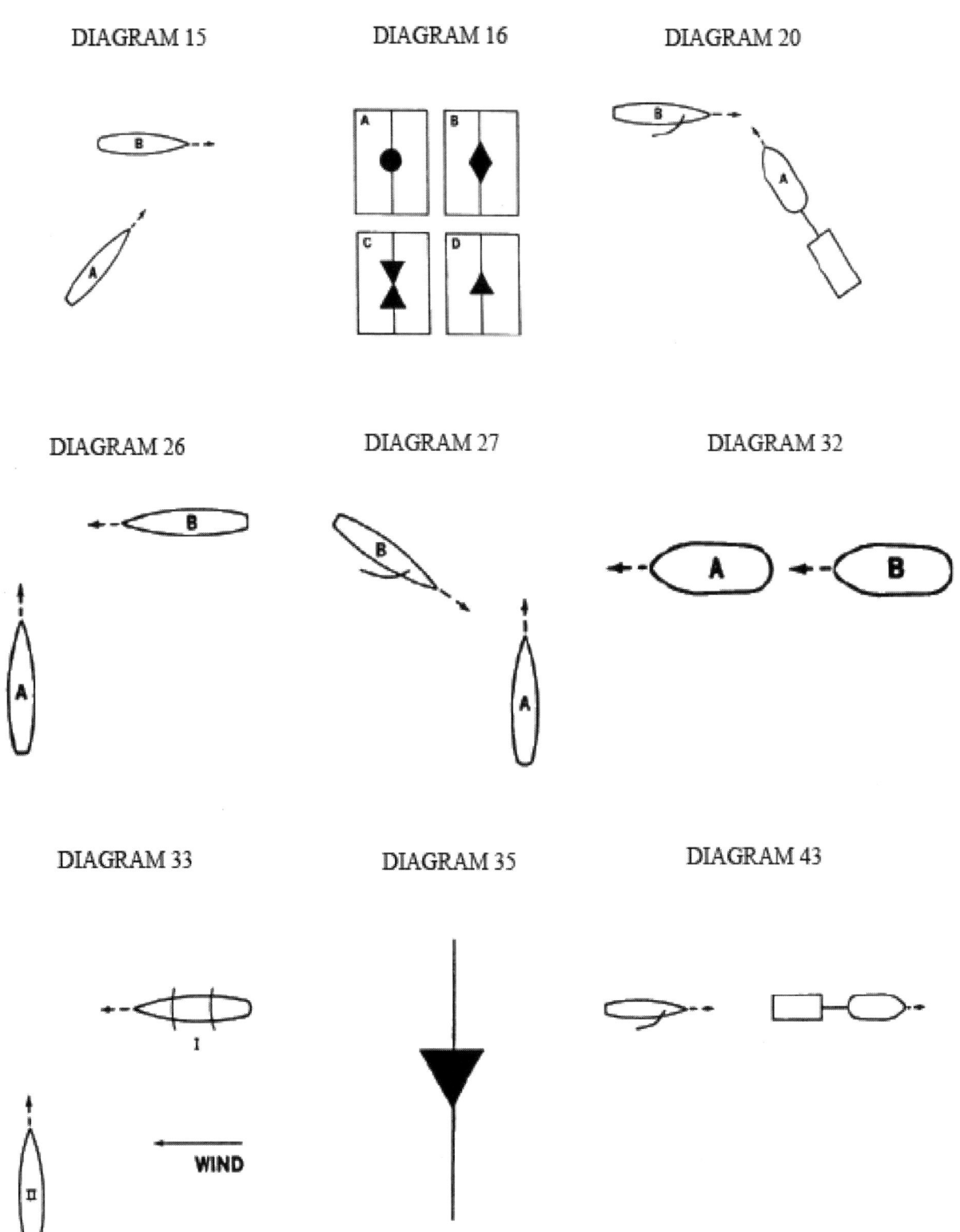

DIAGRAM 15   DIAGRAM 16   DIAGRAM 20

DIAGRAM 26   DIAGRAM 27   DIAGRAM 32

DIAGRAM 33   DIAGRAM 35   DIAGRAM 43

WIND

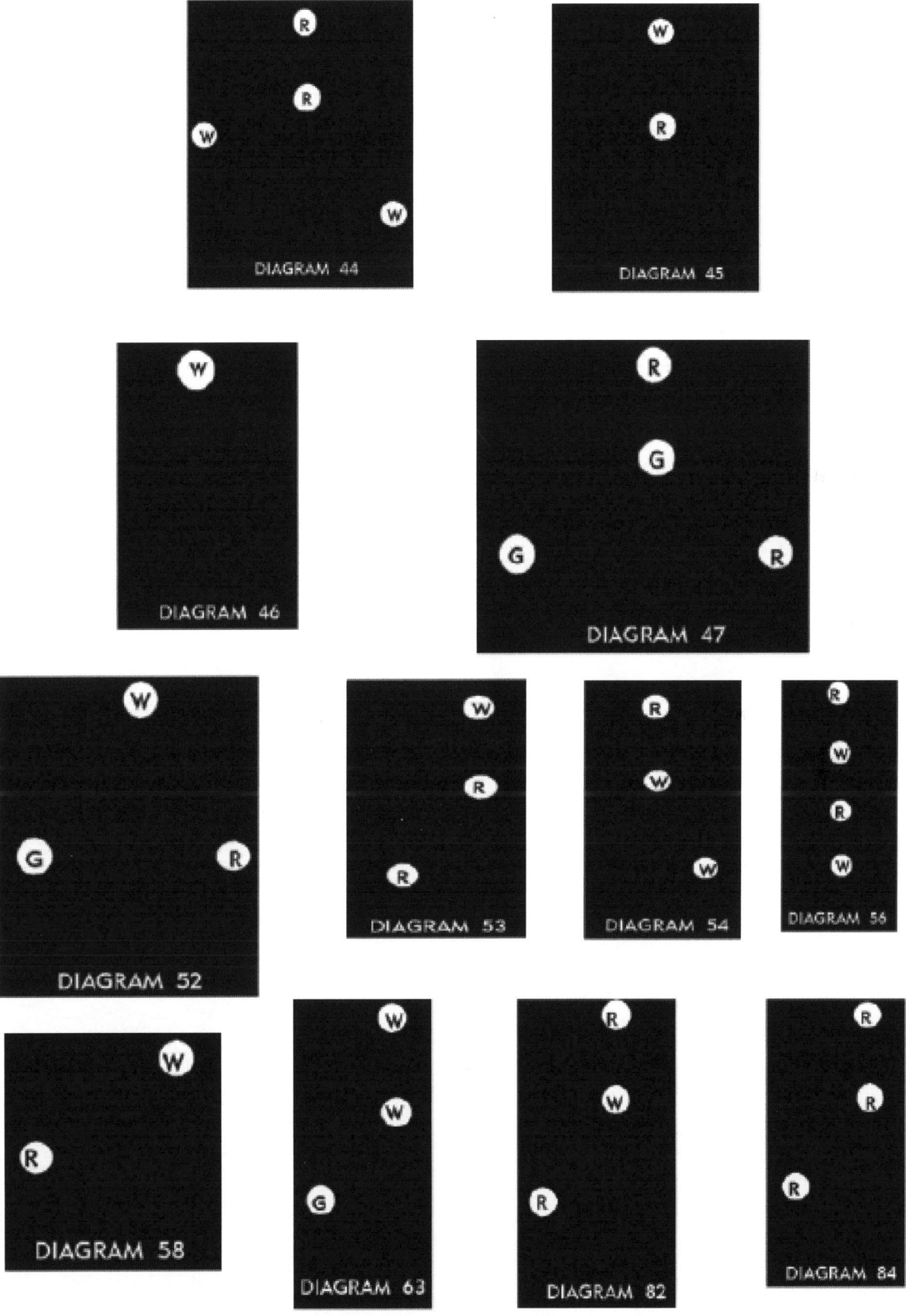

DIAGRAM 44

DIAGRAM 45

DIAGRAM 46

DIAGRAM 47

DIAGRAM 52

DIAGRAM 53

DIAGRAM 54

DIAGRAM 56

DIAGRAM 58

DIAGRAM 63

DIAGRAM 82

DIAGRAM 84

Rules of the Road
Statements to Recognize

Rules of the Road International and Inland

Part A General

Rule 1 Application

Rule 2 Responsibilities

1. There is a provision to depart from the Rules, if necessary, to avoid **immediate danger.**
2. The Rules state that vessels may depart from the Rules when **it is necessary to avoid immediate danger.**
3. According to the Navigation Rules, you may depart from the Rules when **you are in immediate danger.**

Rule 3 General Definitions

4. A vessel is "engaged in fishing" when **she is using fishing apparatus which restricts her maneuverability.**
5. The term "power-driven vessel" refers to any vessel **propelled by machinery.**
6. As defined in the Rules, the term "vessel" includes **all of these**; a seaplane, a non-displacement craft, and a barge.
7. This statement is TRUE concerning a "vessel engaged in fishing"; **the vessel may be using nets, lines, or trawls.**
8. The term "restricted visibility" as used in the Rules refers **to any condition where visibility is restricted.**
9. In order for a vessel to be "engaged in fishing" she must be **using fishing gear which restricts her maneuverability.**
10. The word "vessel", in the Rules, includes **all of these;** sailing ships, non-displacement craft, and seaplanes.
11. **A purse seiner fishing vessel hauling her nets** is "underway" according to the Rules.
12. As defined in the Rules, the term "vessel" includes **all of these**; seaplanes, non-displacement craft, and barges.
13. **A vessel towing unable to deviate from her course** is a vessel "restricted in her ability to maneuver".
14. All of the following vessels are "restricted in their ability to maneuver"; laying a pipeline, dredging, and mineclearing, EXCEPT a vessel **not under command.**
15. **A vessel engaged in underwater operations** is to be regarded as a vessel "restricted in her ability to maneuver".
16. According to the Rules, **a sailing vessel** is NOT "restricted in her ability to maneuver".
17. A vessel which is "restricted in her ability to maneuver" under the Rules, is a vessel which is **engaged in underwater operations.**
18. **A vessel whose anchor is fouled** is NOT classified as "restricted in her ability to maneuver".

Part B Steering and Sailing Rules

Subpart 1 Conduct of Vessels in Any Condition of Visibility

Rule 4 Application

Rule 5 Look-out

19. The rule regarding look-outs applies in **all of these** situations; in restricted visibility, between dusk and dawn, and in heavy traffic.
20. A proper look-out shall be maintained **at all times.**

Rule 6 Safe Speed

21. The Navigation Rules state that a vessel shall be operated at a safe speed at all times so that she can be stopped within **a distance appropriate to the existing circumstances and conditions.**
22. A vessel must proceed at a safe speed **at all times.**
23. **The maneuverability of the vessel** is listed in the Rules as one factor which must be taken into account when determining safe speed.
24. Every vessel should at all times proceed at a "safe speed". "Safe speed" is defined as that speed where **you can take proper and effective action to avoid collision.**

Rule 7 Risk of Collision

25. Risk of collision exists when an approaching vessel has a **generally steady bearing and decreasing range.**
26. **A vessel is on your starboard quarter, range decreasing, bearing is constant** is a situation in which you think a risk of collision exists.
27. **A vessel is on your starboard quarter, range decreasing, bearing is constant** is a situation in which risk of collision would definitely exist.
28. You are watching another vessel approach and her compass bearing is not changing. This means that **a risk of collision exists.**
29. The Rules state that risk of collision shall be deemed to exist **if the bearing of an approaching vessel does not appreciably change.**
30. You are approaching another vessel and are not sure whether danger of collision exists. You must assume **there is risk of collision.**

Rule 8 Action to Avoid Collision

31. When taking action to avoid collision, you should **make sure the action is taken in enough time.**
32. You are approaching another vessel and are not sure if risk of collision exists. You must assume **there is risk of collision.**

33. You are approaching another vessel. She is about one mile distant and is on your starboard bow. You believe she will cross ahead of you. She then sounds a whistle signal of five short blasts. You should **make a large course change, and slow down if necessary.**
34. A vessel shall slacken her speed, stop, or reverse her engines, if necessary, to **avoid collision, allow more time to assess the situation, and be stopped in an appropriate distance**
35. You are approaching another vessel on crossing courses. She is approximately half a mile distant and is presently on your starboard bow. You believe she will cross ahead of you. She then sounds a whistle signal of five short blasts. You should **make a large course change, accompanied by the appropriate whistle signal, and slow down if necessary.**

Rule 9 Narrow Channels

36. Your 15-meter vessel is crossing a narrow channel and a large cargo vessel to port is within the channel and crossing your course. You must **not cross the channel if you might impede the other vessel.**
37. When underway in a channel, you should keep to the **starboard side of the channel.**
38. You are approaching a narrow channel. You see a vessel that can only be navigated safely within the channel. You should **not cross the channel if you might impede the other vessel.**
39. Your 15-meter tug is underway and crossing a deep and narrow channel. A large container vessel is off your port bow on a steady bearing. This statement is TRUE concerning this situation; **you are not to impede the safe passage of the container vessel in the channel.**
40. **All of these vessels** shall NOT impede the passage of a vessel which can safely navigate only within a narrow channel or fairway; a vessel of less than 20 meters in length, a vessel sailing, and a vessel fishing.
41. In narrow channels, vessels of less than **20 meters** shall not impede the safe passage of vessels which can navigate only inside that channel.
42. You are crossing a narrow channel in a 15-meter vessel when you sight a tankship off your port bow coming up the channel. This statement is TRUE; **you shall not impede the safe passage of the tankship.**
43. **A vessel of less than 20 meters in length** is directed not to impede the passage of a vessel which can only navigate inside a narrow channel.

Rule 10 Traffic Separation Schemes

44. A vessel using a traffic separation scheme shall **avoid anchoring in areas near the termination of the scheme.**
45. There are two classes of vessels which, to the extent necessary to carry out their work, do not have to comply with the rule regarding traffic separation schemes. One of these is a vessel **servicing a submarine cable.**

Subpart 2 Application - Vessels in sight of one another

Rule 11 Application

Rule 12 Sailing Vessels

46. If two sailing vessels have the wind on the same side, **the one to windward** must keep clear of the other.
47. This statement is TRUE concerning two sailing vessels; **a sailing vessel with the wind forward of the beam on her port side shall keep out of the way of a sailing vessel with the wind forward of the beam on the starboard side.**
48. If two sailing vessels are running free with the wind on the same side, **the one to windward** must keep clear of the other.
49. Two sailing vessels are approaching each other as shown in Diagram 3. This statement is correct; **Vessel "II" should stand on because she has the wind on her starboard side.**

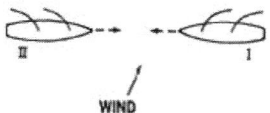

Rule 13 Overtaking

50. A vessel shall be deemed to be overtaking when she can see at night **only the stern light of the vessel.**
51. A sailing vessel is overtaking a tug and tow as shown in Diagram 43. This statement is CORRECT. **The tug is the stand-on vessel because it is being overtaken.**

52. At night you come up on the stern of a vessel and plan to overtake it. You would see **the stern light of the other vessel.**
53. You are on vessel "A" and approaching vessel "B" as shown in Diagram 15. You are not sure whether your vessel is crossing or overtaking vessel "B". You should **consider it to be an overtaking situation.**

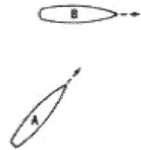

54. While underway at night you are coming up on a vessel from astern. You would you expect to see **one white light.**

55. The Rules state that a vessel overtaking another vessel is relieved of her duty to keep clear when **she is past and clear of the other vessel.**
56. A vessel is overtaking when she can see **only the stern light of the vessel** of a vessel ahead.
57. This statement concerning an overtaking situation is correct; **the overtaking vessel must keep out of the way of the other.**
58. A vessel approaching your vessel from 235° relative is in **an overtaking** situation.

Rule 14 Head-on Situation

59. Two vessels meeting in a "head-on" situation are directed by the Rules to **alter course to starboard and pass port to port.**
60. A "head on" situation shall be deemed to exist at night when a power-driven vessel sees another power-driven vessel ahead and **both sidelights and masthead light(s) are visible.**
61. In this situation the Rules require both vessels to change course; **two power-driven vessels meeting head-on.**
62. Two vessels are approaching each other head on. This action should be taken to avoid collision; **both vessels should alter course to starboard.**
63. A head-on situation at night is one in which you see dead ahead a vessel showing **both sidelights and her masthead lights in line or nearly in line.**
64. Two vessels are meeting head-on. The vessels must pass as follows; **both vessels should alter course to starboard and pass port to port.**
65. This describes a head-on situation; **seeing both sidelights of a vessel directly ahead.**
66. Rule 14 describes the action to be taken by vessels meeting head-on. **all of the following conditions** must exist in order for this rule to apply; both vessels must be power-driven, they must be meeting on reciprocal or nearly reciprocal courses, and the situation must involve risk of collision.
67. Two vessels are approaching each other near head on. This action should be taken to avoid collision; **both vessels should alter course to starboard.**
68. You are on vessel "A" pushing a barge ahead and meeting vessel "B" as shown in Diagram 12. This is how the vessels should pass; **BOTH vessels must alter course to starboard and pass port to port.**

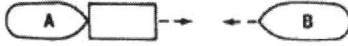

69. Vessel "A" (towing) and vessel "B" are meeting as shown in Diagram 12. In this situation, this statement is TRUE; **both vessels should alter course to starboard and pass port to port.**

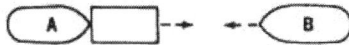

70. While underway at night, you sight a vessel ahead displaying the lights shown in Diagram 52. The vessels should pass as follows; **both vessels should alter course to starboard and pass port to port.**

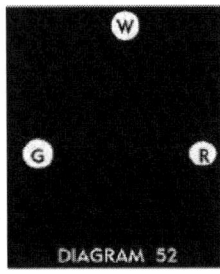

Rule 15 Crossing Situation

71. Vessels "A" and "B" are crossing as shown in Diagram 26. This statement is TRUE; **vessel "A" must keep clear of vessel "B".**

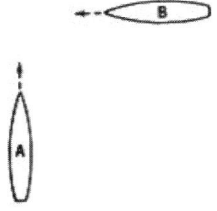

Rule 16 Action by the Give-way Vessel

72. Every vessel that is to keep out of the way of another vessel must take positive early action to comply with this obligation and must **avoid crossing ahead of the other vessel.**
73. In a crossing situation, the vessel which has the other on her own starboard side shall **if the circumstances of the case admit, avoid crossing ahead of the other.**
74. Your vessel is NOT making way, but is not in any way disabled. Another vessel is approaching you on your starboard beam. This statement is TRUE; **your vessel is the give-way vessel in a crossing situation.**

75. Vessel "A" is underway and pushing ahead when vessel "B" is sighted off the starboard bow as shown in Diagram 5. This statement is TRUE; **vessel "B" is the stand-on vessel because it is to starboard of vessel "A".**

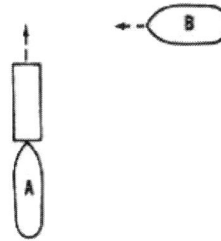

76. As shown in Diagram 5, vessel "A", which is pushing ahead, and vessel "B" are crossing. **Vessel "B" is the stand-on vessel because she is to starboard of vessel "A".**

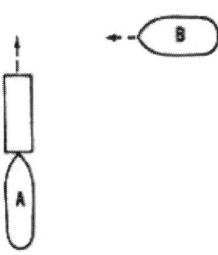

Rule 17 Action by the Stand-on Vessel

77. A stand-on vessel is FIRST allowed by the Rules to take action in order to avoid collision **when the give-way vessel is not taking appropriate action to avoid collision.**
78. If your vessel is the stand-on vessel in a crossing situation **you must keep your course and speed.**
79. If it becomes necessary for a stand-on vessel to take action to avoid collision, she shall NOT, if possible, **turn to port for a vessel on her own port side.**
80. The stand-on vessel shall change course and speed **when action by the give-way vessel alone cannot prevent collision.**
81. In a crossing situation, a stand-on vessel which is forced to take action in order to avoid collision with a vessel on her own port side shall, if possible, avoid **turning to port.**
82. In a crossing situation, the stand-on vessel should normally **maintain course and speed.**
83. For a stand-on vessel to take action to avoid collision she shall, if possible, NOT **turn to port for a vessel on her port side.**
84. You are the watch officer on a power-driven vessel and notice a large sailing vessel approaching from astern. You should **hold your course and speed.**
85. If you are the stand-on vessel in a crossing situation, you may take action to avoid collision by your maneuver alone. This action MAY be taken **when it becomes apparent to you that the give-way vessel is not taking appropriate action.**
86. You are the stand-on vessel in a crossing situation. You may hold your course and speed until **action by the give-way vessel alone will not prevent collision.**
87. **All of these** must be TRUE in order for a stand-on vessel to take action to avoid collision by her maneuver alone; she must be in sight of the give-way vessel, there must be risk of collision, and she must determine that the give-way vessel is not taking appropriate action.

88. Two power-driven vessels are crossing so as to involve risk of collision. This statement is TRUE, according to the Rules; **if the stand-on vessel takes action, she shall avoid changing course to port.**

89. The stand-on vessel in a crossing situation shall take action to avoid the other vessel **when action by the give-way vessel alone will not prevent a collision.**

90. In order for a stand-on vessel to take action in a situation, she must determine that the other vessel **is not taking appropriate action.**

91. You are in charge of a stand-on vessel in a crossing situation. The other vessel is 1.5 miles to port. You believe that risk of collision exists. You should **take avoiding action only after giving the give-way vessel time to take action, and determining that her action is not appropriate.**

92. You are in charge of a power-driven vessel navigating at night. You sight the red sidelight of another vessel on your port bow. The other vessel's after masthead light is to the right of her forward masthead light. You should **hold course and speed.**

Rule 18 Responsibilities between Vessels

93. A power-driven vessel underway shall keep out of the way of **all of these vessels;** not under command, restricted in her ability to maneuver, and engaged in fishing.

94. You are aboard vessel "A", a power-driven vessel and vessel "B", a sailing vessel, is sighted off your port bow as shown in Diagram 27. The stand-on vessel is **vessel "B" because it is a sailing vessel.**

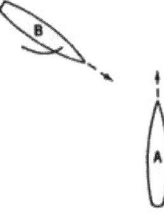

95. In a crossing situation on open waters, a sailing vessel shall keep out of the way of all the following vessels; vessel not under command, vessel restricted in her ability to maneuver, and a vessel fishing, EXCEPT a **power-driven vessel approaching on her starboard side.**

96. In the situation illustrated in Diagram 2, vessel I is a power-driven vessel. Vessel II is a sailing vessel with the wind dead aft. This statement about this situation is correct; **vessel I should keep out of the way of Vessel II.**

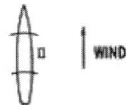

97. You are underway on vessel "A" and sight vessel "B" which is a vessel underway and fishing as shown in Diagram 14. This statement is true; **vessel "A" must keep out of the way of vessel "B" because "B" is fishing.**

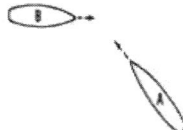

98. **A seaplane** should not impede the navigation of a power-driven vessel.

99. A vessel underway and fishing shall keep out of the way of a **vessel not under command.**

100. The Rules state that a seaplane shall **in general, keep well clear of all vessels.**

101. On open waters, a power-driven vessel shall keep out of the way of a **sailing vessel.**

102. A power-driven vessel has on her port side a sailing vessel which is on a collision course. The power-driven vessel is required to **keep clear.**

103. This statement is TRUE concerning seaplanes on the water; **a seaplane on the water shall, in general, keep well clear of all vessels.**

104. You are aboard vessel "A", a power-driven vessel, on open waters and vessel "B", a sailing vessel, is sighted off your port bow as shown in Diagram 27. This vessel is the stand-on vessel; **vessel "B" because it is sailing.**

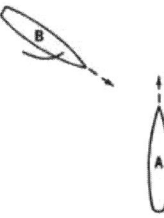

105. You are aboard vessel "A" which is towing on open waters when vessel "B", a sailing vessel, is sighted off your port bow as shown in Diagram 20. **Vessel "B" is the stand-on vessel because it is sailing.**

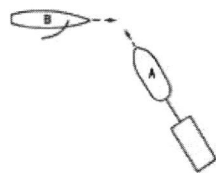

106. Vessels I and II are underway as shown in Diagram 33. Vessel I is a sailing vessel with the wind dead aft. Vessel II is a power-driven vessel trawling. This statement is TRUE; **vessel I is to keep clear because the other vessel is fishing.**

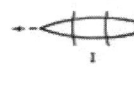

WIND

Rule 19 Conduct of Vessels in Restricted Visibility

107.   You are on watch in the fog. Your vessel is proceeding at a safe speed when you hear a fog signal ahead of you. The Rules require you to navigate with caution and, if danger of collision exists, **reduce to bare steerageway.**

108.   You are underway in restricted visibility. You hear the fog signal of another vessel about 22° on your starboard bow. If danger of collision exists you must **reduce your speed to bare steerageway.**

109.   You are making way in restricted visibility and hear a fog signal forward of the beam. Nothing appears on your radar screen. You must **slow to bare steerageway.**

110.   You are on a power-driven vessel in fog. Your vessel is proceeding at a safe speed when you hear a fog signal ahead of you. The Rules require you to navigate with caution and, if danger of collision exists **reduce to bare steerageway.**

111.   While underway in fog, you hear the fog signal of another vessel ahead. If a risk of collision exists, you must **slow to bare steerageway and navigate with caution.**

112.   You hear the fog signal of another vessel forward of your beam. Risk of collision may exist. You MUST **reduce speed to bare steerageway.**

113.   When navigating in restricted visibility, a power-driven vessel shall **have her engines ready for immediate maneuver.**

114.   Your vessel is underway in reduced visibility. You hear the fog signal of another vessel about 30° on your starboard bow. If danger of collision exists, you must **reduce your speed to bare steerageway.**

115.   This statement concerning maneuvering in restricted visibility is FALSE; **a vessel which hears a fog signal forward of her beam shall stop her engines.**

Part C Lights and Shapes

Rule 20 Application

116.   The rules concerning lights shall be complied with in all weathers from sunset to sunrise. The lights **shall be displayed in restricted visibility during daylight hours.**

117.   Day-shapes MUST be shown **during daylight hours.**

Rule 21 Definitions

118.   The arc of visibility for sidelights is from right ahead to **22.5° abaft the beam.**

119.   A towing light, according to the Rules, is a **yellow light.**

120.   You see a vessel's green sidelight bearing due east from you. The vessel might be heading **southwest (225°).**

121.   The stern light shall be positioned such that it will show from dead astern to **67.5** degrees on each side of the stern of the vessel.

122.   A vessel is towing and carrying the required masthead lights. The visibility arc of these masthead lights is **225.0°.**

123.   A "flashing light", by the definition given in the rules, is a light that **flashes at regular intervals at a frequency of 120 flashes or more per minute.**

124.   You see a red sidelight bearing NW (315°). That vessel may be heading **south (180°).**

Rule 22 Visibilities of Lights

Rule 23 Power-driven Vessels Underway

125. The minimum length of a power-driven vessel that must show forward and after masthead lights is **50 meters.**

126. The minimum vessel length which must show a second masthead light abaft of and higher than the forward one is **50 meters.**

127. The lights shown in Diagram 58 are those of a **power-driven vessel of less than 50 meters in length.**

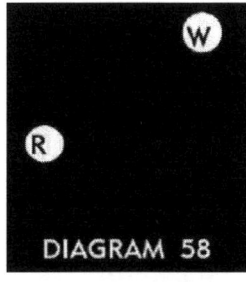

128. The maximum length of a power-driven vessel which may show an all-round white light and sidelights instead of a masthead light, sidelights and a stern light is **11.9 meters.**

129. A self-propelled dredge not engaged in dredging but proceeding to a dredging location at night would **be required to show the lights of a power-driven vessel underway.**

130. Your tug is underway at night and NOT towing. The light your vessel should show aft to other vessels coming up from astern is **one white light.**

131. A power-driven vessel exhibits the same lights as a **pushing vessel and a vessel being pushed, when they are in a composite unit.**

132. At night, a power-driven vessel less than 12 meters in length may, instead of the normal navigation lights, show sidelights and one **white light.**

133. At night, a vessel displaying the lights shown in Diagram 52 is **underway.**

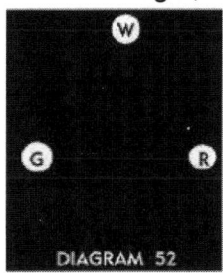

134. A 30-meter tug is underway and NOT towing. At night, this vessel must show sidelights and **one masthead light and a stern light.**

135. A towing vessel pushing a barge ahead and rigidly connected in a composite unit shall show the lights of **a power-driven vessel, not towing.**

136. The masthead light may be located at other than the fore and aft centerline on a power-driven vessel **less than 12 meters in length.**

137.   The lights shown in Diagram 52 are those of a **power-driven vessel of less than 50 meters in length.**

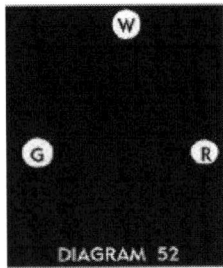

138.   You see a vessel displaying ONLY the lights shown in Diagram 45. This could be a **pilot vessel less than 50 meters, underway and NOT engaged on pilotage duty.**

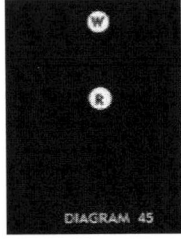

139.   You see the lights shown in Diagram 45. It would be the **port side of a power driven vessel.**

140.   A vessel which is underway at night and displaying the lights shown in Diagram 52 is **a power driven vessel under 50 meters.**

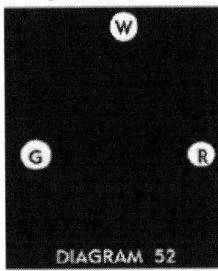

Rule 24 Towing and Pushing

141.   A towing vessel 35 meters in length, with a tow 100 meters astern, must show a minimum of **2** masthead lights.

142.   This vessel must exhibit three white masthead lights in a vertical line; **a vessel whose tow exceeds 200 meters astern.**

143.   A vessel displaying the day shape shown in Diagram 10 is **towing.**

144.   A vessel that is not equipped with towing lights should show that it has a vessel in tow by **shining a searchlight on the towline of the towed vessel.**
145.   At night you are towing a barge astern, if any, the lights the barge you are towing should display are **sidelights and a stern light.**
146.   A towing vessel 30 meters in length is pushing barges ahead. The number of white masthead lights the vessel is REQUIRED to show at night is **two.**
147.   A vessel being towed astern, at night, will show **sidelights and a stern light.**
148.   The day-shape lettered **B** shown in Diagram 16 indicates a vessel with a tow exceeding 200 meters in length.

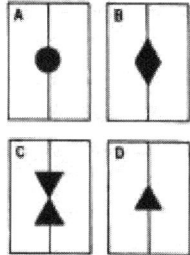

149.   A vessel being towed astern shall show at night **sidelights and a stern light.**
150.   A vessel being towed astern, where the length of the tow exceeds 200 meters, will exhibit **a diamond shape where it can best be seen.**
151.   A power-driven vessel, when towing astern, shall show **a towing light in a vertical line above the stern light.**
152.   **Side lights and a stern light** must be shown on a barge being towed astern at night.
153.   A power-driven vessel, when towing astern, shall show **a towing light in a vertical line above the stern light.**
154.   An inconspicuous, partly submerged vessel or object being towed, where the length of tow is 100 meters, shall show **a diamond shape.**
155.   A single towing light will be carried above a vessel's stern light **only if she is towing astern.**
156.   The light(s), if any, you would show at night if your vessel was broken down and being towed astern by another vessel are **the colored sidelights and a white stern light.**
157.   A vessel, which does not normally engage in towing operations, is towing a vessel in distress. She **need not show the lights for a vessel engaged in towing, if it is impractical to do so.**
158.   A 20-meter vessel is towing another vessel astern. The length of the tow from the stern of the towing vessel to the stern of the tow is 75 meters. The number of white towing masthead lights the towing vessel shall show at night is **2.**
159.   A power-driven vessel with a 150-meter stern tow shall display **a towing light above the stern light.**

160. At night, you are towing a partly submerged vessel, 20 meters in length and 4 meters in breadth. The lights you must display on the towed vessel are **a white light at the forward end and a white light at the after end.**

161. The lights, if any, you would exhibit at night if your vessel were broken down and being towed by another vessel are **the colored sidelights and a white stern light.**

162. **A diamond** day-shape must be shown on a partly submerged vessel which is being towed.

163. A vessel being towed astern, where the length of the tow exceeds 200 meters, will exhibit **a diamond shape where it can best be seen.**

164. You are towing two barges astern. The length of the tow from the stern of the tug to the stern of the last barge is 150 meters. The number of white towing identification lights should be displayed on the tugboat at night is **2.**

165. You are overtaking a vessel at night and you see a yellow light showing above the stern light of the overtaken vessel. The overtaken vessel is **towing astern.**

166. A power-driven vessel towing another vessel astern (tow less than 200 meters) shall show **two masthead lights in a vertical line instead of either the forward or after masthead lights.**

167. A vessel towed astern shall show **sidelights and a stern light.**

168. At night, a broken down vessel being towed would show the same lights as **a barge.**

169. Two barges are being pushed ahead by a tugboat. This statement is TRUE concerning lights on the barges; **the barges should be lighted as one vessel.**

170. You are approaching another vessel at night. You can see both red and green sidelights and, above the level of the sidelights, three white lights in a vertical line. The vessel may be **towing a tow more than 200 meters astern.**

171. When towing more than one barge astern at night **each barge in the tow must be lighted.**

172. In Diagram 16 the day-shape shown by letter **B** indicates a vessel with a tow exceeding 200 meters in length.

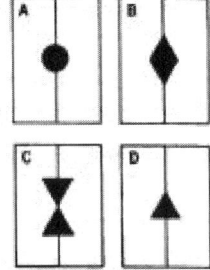

173. A vessel displaying the lights shown Diagram 63 is **towing astern.**

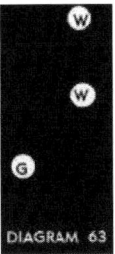

174. A vessel displaying the day-shape shown in Diagram 10 **has a tow that exceeds 200 meters in length.**

Rule 25 Sailing Vessels Underway and Vessels Under Oars

175. A vessel 15 meters in length which is proceeding under sail as well as being propelled by machinery shall exhibit during the daytime **a cone with its apex downward.**
176. A 22-meter sailing vessel when also being propelled by machinery shall show during daylight hours a **black cone apex down.**
177. A sailing vessel displaying the day-shape shown in Diagram 35 is indicating that she is **being propelled by power as well as sail.**

178. A vessel which is underway at night and displaying the lights shown in Diagram 47 is **sailing.**

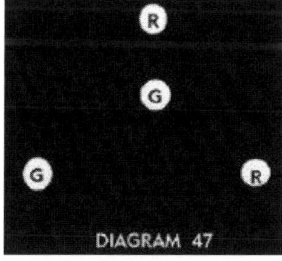

179. A sailing vessel is NOT allowed to show the all-round red over green lights on the mast if **her sidelights and stern light are combined in one lantern and shown on the mast.**
180. A 15-meter sailing vessel would be required to show **sidelights, and stern light, but they may be in a combined lantern on the mast.**
181. If a rowboat underway does NOT show the lights specified for a sailing vessel underway, it shall show a **white light shown in sufficient time to prevent collision.**
182. A sailing vessel underway may exhibit **a red light over a green light at the masthead.**
183. A sailing vessel of over 20 meters in length underway <u>must</u> show a **stern light.**
184. A 20-meter sailing vessel underway must exhibit a **stern light.**
185. At night you sight a vessel displaying one green light. This light could indicate a **sailboat underway.**

186.   At night, a vessel displaying the light shown in Diagram 46 is **sailing.**

Rule 26 Fishing Vessels

187.   A vessel displaying the lights shown in Diagram 82 is a **fishing vessel.**

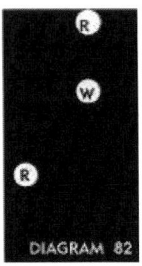

188.   A vessel engaged in fishing should display the day signals lettered **B** shown Diagram 1.

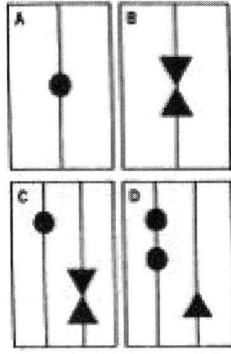

189.   At night, you would see **a red light over a white light** on a vessel engaged in fishing, other than trawling.

190.   A vessel trawling will display a **green light over a white light.**

191.   If a vessel is engaged in fishing according to the definitions in the Rules, it will have **gear that restricts maneuverability.**

192.   A vessel engaged in fishing, and at anchor, shall show **a red light over a white light, whether underway or at anchor.**

193.   A vessel which is fishing must show sidelights and a stern light only when **underway and making way.**

194.   A vessel at night, displaying the lights shown in Diagram 82 is **fishing.**

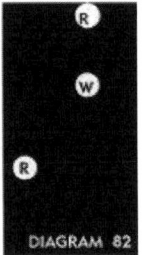

195. A vessel engaged in fishing must display a light in the direction of any gear that extends outward more than 150 meters. The color of this light is **white.**

196. **A fishing vessel that is <u>not making way</u> shall NOT show her sidelights.**

197. A vessel displaying the lights shown in Diagram 54 is a **fishing vessel.**

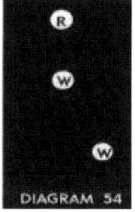

198. At night a vessel displaying the lights shown in Diagram 82 is **engaged in fishing.**

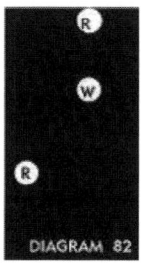

Rule 27 Vessels Not Under Command or Vessels Restricted in Their Ability to Maneuver

199. During the day, a dredge will indicate the side on which it is safe to pass by displaying **two diamonds in a vertical line.**

200. A power-driven vessel "not under command" at night must show **two red** lights in a vertical line.

201. A vessel displaying the lights shown in Diagram 84 is **not under command.**

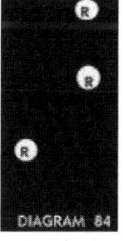

202. **A vessel restricted in her ability to maneuver** would show 3 day-shapes in a vertical line, the highest and lowest being balls and the middle shape being a diamond.

203. At night, **two green lights** are required to be shown by a dredge on the side of the dredge which another vessel may pass.

204. Two all-round red lights displayed in a vertical line are shown by a vessel **not under command.**

205. A vessel displaying the day-shapes shown in Diagram 7 is **broken down.**

206. **A vessel mineclearing** is a "vessel restricted in her ability to maneuver" under the Rules.
207. **A vessel not under command** would have no white lights visible when meeting her head-on.
208. A vessel which is unable to maneuver due to some exceptional circumstance shall show two red lights in a vertical line and **when making way at night, sidelights and a stern light.**
209. A vessel displaying the day signal shown in Diagram 7 is **not under command.**

210. While underway, you see a vessel displaying the day-shapes shown in Diagram 6. The action which should be taken is to; **stay clear, the other vessel is maneuvering with difficulty.**

211. A rigid replica of the International Code flag "A" may be shown by a vessel **engaged in diving operations.**
212. A vessel towing astern in an operation which severely restricts the towing vessel and her tow in their ability to deviate from their course shall show **all of these** lights when making way; the masthead lights for a towing vessel, the lights for a vessel restricted in its ability to maneuver, and sidelights, stern light and towing light.
213. An anchored vessel is servicing an aid to navigation and is restricted in her ability to maneuver. The lights she will show are **three lights in a vertical line, the highest and lowest red and the middle white, and anchor lights.**
214. **Masthead lights, sidelights and stern light** are shown by a "vessel restricted in her ability to maneuver" to indicate that the vessel is making way.
215. **A vessel engaged in diving operations** may show three lights in a vertical line, the top and bottom being red and the middle being white.

216.   A vessel engaged in a towing operation such as severely restricts the towing vessel and her tow in their ability to deviate from their course shall carry **the lights for a towing vessel and the lights for a vessel restricted in her ability to maneuver.**

217.   A vessel engaged in mineclearing shows **all of these** special identity lights; in addition to the lights required for a power-driven vessel, which mean that other vessels should not approach within 1000 meters of the mine clearing vessel, and which are green and show all-round the horizon.

218.   A vessel not under command making way at night would show **two all-round red lights in a vertical line, sidelights, and a stern light.**

219.   A vessel displaying the lights shown in Diagram 56 could be a vessel **underway and laying cable.**

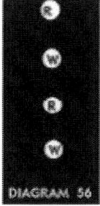

220.   A vessel transferring provisions or cargo at sea shall display during the day **three black shapes in a vertical line; the highest and lowest shall be balls and the middle one a diamond**

221.   You see a vessel displaying the day signal shown in Diagram 6. The vessel may be **laying cable.**

Rule 28 Vessels Constrained by Their Draft

Rule 29 Pilot Vessels

222.   A vessel displaying ONLY the lights shown in Diagram 53 is a **vessel engaged on pilotage duty underway.**

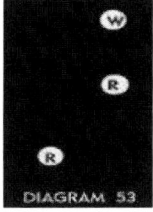

Rule 30 Anchored Vessels and Vessels Aground

223.   The lights displayed in Diagram 44 would be shown by a vessel which is **aground.**

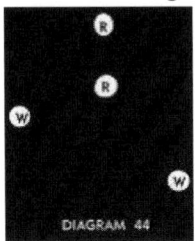

224.   A vessel at anchor shall display, between sunrise and sunset, on the forward part of the vessel where it can best be seen **one black ball.**

225.   A vessel displaying the day-shapes shown in Diagram 11 is **aground.**

226.   Working lights shall be used to illuminate the decks of a vessel **over 100 meters at anchor.**

227.   When anchoring a 25-meter vessel at night, you must show **one all-round white light.**

228.   **Three black balls** is the day-shape a vessel aground would show during daylight.

229.   **Three black balls** is the day-shape which must be shown by a vessel 25 meters in length aground during daylight hours.

230.   A vessel aground at night is required to show two red lights in a vertical line as well as **anchor lights.**

231.   A vessel 30 meters in length and aground would display a day-shape consisting of **three black balls in a vertical line.**

232.   **Three black balls** would be the signal a vessel aground would show during daylight.

233.   At night, a vessel which is less than 7 meters in length and anchored in an area where other vessels do not normally navigate is **not required to show any anchor lights.**

234.   **All of these** statements are TRUE concerning a vessel of 75 meters in length, at anchor; she must show an all-round white light forward, she must show a second all-round white light aft, and she may use her working lights to illuminate her decks.

235.   An anchor ball need NOT be exhibited by an anchored vessel if she is **less than 7 meters in length, and not in or near an area where other vessels normally navigate.**

Rule 31 Seaplanes

Part D Sound and Light Signals

Rule 32 Definitions

236.   The term "prolonged blast" means a blast of from **four to six seconds.**

237.   A "short blast" on the whistle has a duration of **1 second.**

238.   Each prolonged blast on whistle signals used by a power-driven vessel in fog, whether making way or underway but not making way, is **four to six seconds.**

239.   The duration of a "short blast" on the whistle is **1 second.**

240.   You are underway and approaching a bend in the channel where vessels approaching from the opposite direction cannot be seen. You should sound **one blast, 4 to 6 seconds in duration.**

Rule 33 Equipment for Sound Signals

241.   **Any vessel over 100 meters** must have a gong, or other equipment which will make the sound of a gong.

242.   This statement is TRUE regarding equipment for sound signals; **manual sounding of the bell and gong must always be possible.**

Rule 34 Maneuvering and Warning Signals

243.   Your vessel is approaching a bend. You hear a prolonged blast from around the bend. You should **answer with one prolonged blast.**

244.   If you do NOT understand the course or intention of an approaching vessel you should sound **at least five short and rapid blasts.**

245.   The whistle signal for a vessel operating astern propulsion is **three short blasts.**

246.   A vessel nearing a bend or an area of a channel or fairway where other vessels may be obscured by an intervening obstruction shall sound **one prolonged blast.**

247.   **Five short and rapid blasts of the whistle** indicate doubt that sufficient action is being taken by another vessel to avoid collision.

248.   The use of the signal consisting of five or more short blasts on the ship's whistle **indicates doubt as to the other vessel's action.**

249.   You are on a vessel nearing a bend in the channel where, because of the height of the bank, you cannot see a vessel approaching from the opposite direction. You should sound **one prolonged blast.**

250.   While underway your vessel approaches a bend in a river where, due to the bank, you cannot see around the bend. You should **sound one prolonged blast.**

251.   The use of the danger signal **indicates doubt as to another vessels actions.**

252.   A whistle signal of three short blasts means **"I am operating astern propulsion".**

253.   A light signal consisting of three flashes means **"I am operating astern propulsion".**

254. **All of these** vessels may use the danger signal; the vessel to starboard when two power-driven vessels are crossing, a vessel engaged in fishing, crossing the course of a sailing vessel, and either of two power-driven vessels meeting head-on.

255. You are approaching a bend in a river where, due to the bank, you cannot see around the other side. A vessel on the other side of the bend sounds one prolonged blast. You should **sound a prolonged blast.**

256. In a crossing situation, **either vessel** may sound the danger signal.

257. A light signal of three flashes means **"I am operating astern propulsion".**

258. While underway and in sight of another vessel you put your engines on astern propulsion. This statement concerning whistle signals is TRUE; **you must sound three short blasts on the whistle.**

259. You are on vessel "A" in Diagram 32, and hear vessel "B" sound a signal indicating her intention to overtake you. You feel it is not safe for vessel "B" to overtake you at the present time. You should **sound five or more short rapid blasts.**

Rule 35 Sound Signals in Restricted Visibility

260. While underway in fog, you hear a prolonged blast from another vessel. This signal indicates a **power-driven vessel underway making way.**

261. A 200-meter vessel is aground in fog. **A whistle signal** is optional.

262. Your vessel is underway but stopped and making no way through the water when fog sets in. The fog signal which you should sound is **two prolonged blasts on the whistle.**

263. A power-driven vessel is underway not making way in the fog. She must sound **two prolonged blasts** at not more than two minute intervals.

264. You are underway, in fog, when you hear a whistle signal of one prolonged blast followed by two short blasts. This signal could indicate a vessel **not under command.**

265. While underway in fog, you hear a short blast, a prolonged blast, and a short blast of a whistle. This signal indicates a **vessel anchored in fog.**

266. A vessel aground in fog shall sound, in addition to the proper anchor signal, **three strokes on the bell before and after the anchor signal.**

267. While underway in fog you hear another vessel sounding two prolonged blasts every two minutes. This signal indicates a power driven vessel **drifting.**

268. **All of these** vessels are required to sound a fog signal of one prolonged followed by two short blasts; a vessel not under command, a sailing vessel underway, and a vessel restricted in its ability to maneuver at anchor.

269. While underway and towing, your vessel enters fog. You should sound **one prolonged blast and two short blasts.**

270. A sailing vessel with the wind abaft the beam is navigating in restricted visibility. She should sound **one prolonged and two short blasts.**

271. You are making headway in fog and hear a fog signal of two prolonged blasts on your starboard quarter. You should **hold your course and speed.**

272. You are underway in fog when you hear the rapid ringing of a bell for five seconds followed by the sounding of a gong for five seconds. This signal indicates a vessel **more than 100 meters in length, at anchor.**

273. While underway, in fog, you hear a whistle signal of one prolonged blast followed by two short blasts. This signal is sounded by a vessel **not under command.**

274. A power-driven vessel making way through the water sounds a fog signal of **one prolonged blast at intervals of not more than two minutes.**

275. In restricted visibility, a vessel fishing with nets shall sound at intervals of two minutes **one prolonged followed by two short blasts.**

276. The optional whistle signal which may be sounded by a vessel at anchor is **one short, one prolonged, followed by one short blast.**

277. Fog bell signals for vessels at anchor or aground shall be sounded at intervals of not more than **1 minute.**

278. You are underway in fog and you hear three distinct bell strokes followed by five seconds of rapid bell ringing followed by three distinct bell strokes. This signal indicates a vessel **aground.**

279. While underway in fog you hear the rapid ringing of a bell. This signal indicates **a vessel at anchor.**

280. You are at anchor in fog on a 120-meter power-driven vessel. You hear the fog signal of a vessel approaching off your port bow. You may sound **one short, one prolonged, and one short blast.**

281. A vessel engaged in fishing underway sounds the same fog signal as a **vessel restricted in her ability to maneuver.**

282. A sailing vessel in fog should sound **one prolonged and two short blasts.**

283. In fog, you hear apparently forward of your beam a fog signal of 2 prolonged blasts in succession every two minutes. This signal indicates a **power-driven vessel underway but stopped and making no way through the water.**

284. If your vessel is underway in fog and you hear one prolonged and three short blasts, this is a **vessel being towed (manned).**

285. A sailing vessel with the wind abaft the beam is navigating in fog. She should sound **one prolonged and two short blasts.**

286. You are in charge of a 120-meter power-driven vessel <u>at anchor</u> in fog, sounding the required anchor signals. You hear the fog signal of a vessel underway off your port bow. You may sound **one short, one prolonged, and one short blast.**

287. While underway in fog you hear a whistle signal consisting of one prolonged blast followed immediately by two short blasts. This signal is sounded in fog by **vessels underway and towing.**

288. A power-driven vessel making way through the water sounds **one prolonged blast every two minutes.**

289. **All of these** vessels are required to sound a fog signal of one prolonged followed by two short blasts; a vessel not under command, a sailing vessel underway, a vessel restricted in its ability to maneuver at anchor.

290. Your vessel is at anchor in fog. The fog signal of another vessel, apparently underway, has been growing louder and the danger of collision appears to exist. In addition to your fog signal, **one short, one prolonged, and one short whistle blast** may be used to indicate your presence.

291. You are underway in a fog when you hear a whistle signal of one prolonged blast followed by two short blasts. This signal could indicate all of the following EXCEPT a vessel **being towed.**

292. A 95-meter vessel aground sounds **a rapid ringing of a bell for 5 seconds, preceded and followed by three separate and distinct strokes on the bell.**

293. While underway in fog you hear a vessel sound one prolonged blast followed by two short blasts. This signal indicates **a vessel towing.**

294. You are underway in fog and you hear one prolonged blast followed by two short blasts. This is a vessel **towing.**

295. In a dense fog, you hear a whistle signal of one prolonged blast followed by three short blasts. This signal is sounded by a **manned vessel being towed.**

296. While underway your vessel enters fog. You stop your engines and the vessel is dead in the water. The fog signal you should sound is **two prolonged blasts every two minutes.**

297. In restricted visibility, a vessel restricted in her ability to maneuver, at anchor, would sound a fog signal of **one prolonged and two short blasts every two minutes.**

298. While underway and pushing a barge ahead, your vessel enters a heavy rain storm. You should sound **one prolonged and two short blasts every two minutes.**

299. While underway in a fog you hear a signal of three strokes of a bell, a rapid ringing of the bell, and three more strokes of the bell. This signal is made by a vessel **aground.**

300. The wind is ESE, and a sailing vessel is steering NW. She should sound **one prolonged and two short blasts at two-minute intervals.**

301. A fog signal of one short, one prolonged, and one short blast may be sounded by a **vessel at anchor.**

302. A power-driven vessel underway in fog making NO way must sounds **two prolonged blasts.**

303. A vessel sounding a fog signal of one short, one prolonged, and one short blast is indicating that the vessel is **at anchor.**

304. If your vessel is underway in fog and you hear one prolonged and three short blasts, this indicates a **vessel being towed.**

305. A tug is towing three manned barges in line in fog. The third vessel of the tow should sound **one prolonged and three short blasts.**

Rule 36 Signals to Attract Attention

Rule 37 Distress Signals

306. **A flaming barrel of oil on deck** is a distress signal.

307. You can indicate that your vessel is in distress by **continuously sounding the fog whistle.**

308. All of the following are distress signals; the continuous sounding of any fog signal apparatus, firing a gun at intervals of about a minute, and a barrel with burning oil in it on deck, EXCEPT **giving five or more short and rapid blasts of the whistle.**

309. A continuous sounding of a fog-signal apparatus indicates **the vessel is in distress.**

310. An orange flag showing a black circle and square is a **distress signal.**

311. According to the rules, **flames on the vessel as from a burning tar barrel** is a distress signal.

312. A man aboard a vessel, signaling by raising and lowering his outstretched arms to each side, is indicating **a distress signal.**

313. Distress signals may be **any of these;** red flares, smoke signals, or sound signals.

314. **Flames on a vessel as from a burning tar barrel** is a distress signal.

315. **A diamond shape where it can best be seen** is NOT a distress signal.

316. **Five or more short rapid blasts on the whistle** is NOT a distress signal.

317.   You are underway and hear a vessel continuously sounding her fog whistle. This indicates the other vessel **is in distress.**

318.   When a vessel signals her distress by means of a gun or other explosive signal, the firing should be at intervals of approximately **1 minute.**

319.   Distress signals may be **any of these** red flares, smoke signals, and sound signals.

320.   All of the following are distress signals under the Rules; orange-colored smoke, red flares, and the repeated raising and lowering of outstretched arms, EXCEPT **a green star signal.**

Navigation General Near Coastal

Meteorology and Oceanography

Weather

Weather is the state of the Earth's atmosphere with respect to temperature, humidity, precipitation, visibility, cloudiness, and other factors. Most weather refers, generally, to the day-to-day temperature and precipitation activity, whereas climate refers to the average long-term meteorological conditions of a place or region. All weather may be traced to the effect of the sun on the earth. Most changes in weather are driven by the temperature and moisture (density) differences between one place and another. The two processes that cause the changes in density are advection and convection. Simply put, convection is the loss or gain of heat resulting from the vertical movement of air. Advection is the loss or gain of heat resulting from the horizontal movement of air.

Weather is of vital importance to the mariner. The wind and state of the sea affect dead reckoning. Reduced visibility limits piloting. The state of the atmosphere affects electronic navigation and radio communication. If the skies are overcast, celestial observations are not available and under certain conditions refraction and dip are disturbed. When wind was the primary motive power, knowledge of the areas of favorable winds was of great importance. Modern vessels are still affected considerably by wind and sea.

Wind

Wind is air in motion. It is the result of horizontal differences in air pressure, which are attributable both to differences of temperature and the nature of the motion itself. In

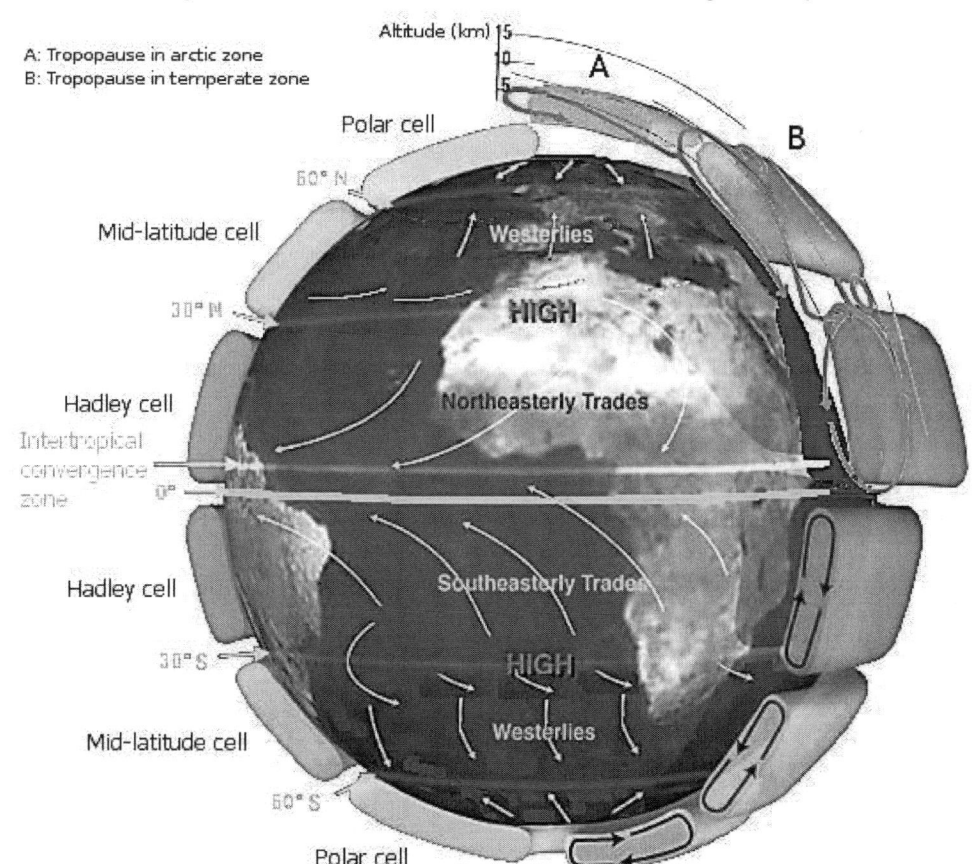

meteorology, winds are often referred to according to their strength, and the direction from which the wind is blowing. Short burst of high speed winds are called gust. Strong winds of intermediate duration are called squalls. Long-term winds have names associated with their average strength, such as, breeze, gale, storm, hurricane and typhoon. Local breezes generated by the heating and cooling of land surfaces may take place on a daily basis. A Land Breeze is a breeze blowing from cooled land areas to replace the rising warm air over nearby warmer water areas. A Sea Breeze is a breeze blowing from cool water that replaces the rising warm air over adjacent land areas.

Air Masses

Most mariners living in the middle latitudes have experienced hot humid summer heat waves and frigid winter cold waves. In the first case, after several days of hot weather, the spell may come to an abrupt end that is marked by thunderstorms and followed by a few days of cool relief. In the second case, thick stratus clouds and snow may replace the clear skies that prevailed, and temperatures may climb to standards that seem milder compared to what preceded them. In both examples, what was

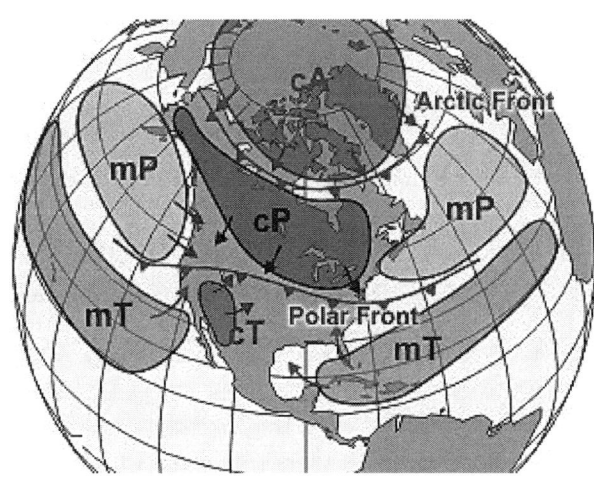

experienced was a period of generally uniform weather conditions followed by a brief period of change and a subsequent reestablishment of a new set of weather conditions that remain for perhaps several days before changing again.

The weather patterns just described are the result of the movements of large bodies of air called air masses. In meteorology, an air mass is a volume of air defined by its temperature and water vapor content. Because of the great variety of physical characteristics found on the earth's surface and, in particular, the contrasts between ocean and land areas, the air overlying these surfaces takes on differing amounts of heat and moisture. The processes of radiation and convection in the lower portions of the atmosphere act in different ways in a number of well-defined regions of the earth. The air overlying these regions takes on characteristics that are common to the particular area, but contrasting to those of other areas. Each distinctive part of the atmosphere where certain common characteristics prevail over a reasonably large area is called an air mass.

High and Low Pressure Systems

Air Pressure, or barometric pressure, is a measure of the force resulting from the weight of a column of air reaching from the earth's surface to the top of the atmosphere over any given area. This is read by an instrument called a Barometer. Not only is the pressure important but so is the change in pressure. A rapid drop in barometric pressure indicates that stormy weather is probable. In an Aneroid Barometer, changes in air pressure cause compression or expansion of a metal diaphragm in the instrument which moves a pointer. To aid in determining the change in the pressure, there is a set hand that can be adjusted to show the pressure change.

Cyclones and Anticyclones

An area of relatively low barometric pressure that contains a rotating air mass which is roughly circular in shape is called a cyclone. Its counterpart, an air mass with high barometric pressure, is called an anticyclone. These terms are generally used when referring to the winds that are associated with air masses.

Cyclones and anticyclones exist as a direct result of the earth's rotation. The winds generated by these moving air masses are deflected toward the right in the northern hemisphere and toward the left in the southern hemisphere. Because of the rotation of the earth and the Coriolis Effect the circulation of air masses tends to be counterclockwise around areas of low pressure and clockwise around areas of high pressure in the northern hemisphere and the opposite rotation south of the equator. The speed of these winds as shown on a weather map is directly related to the spacing of the isobars. Isobars are lines drawn on a weather map to connect all points that have the same barometric pressure readings.

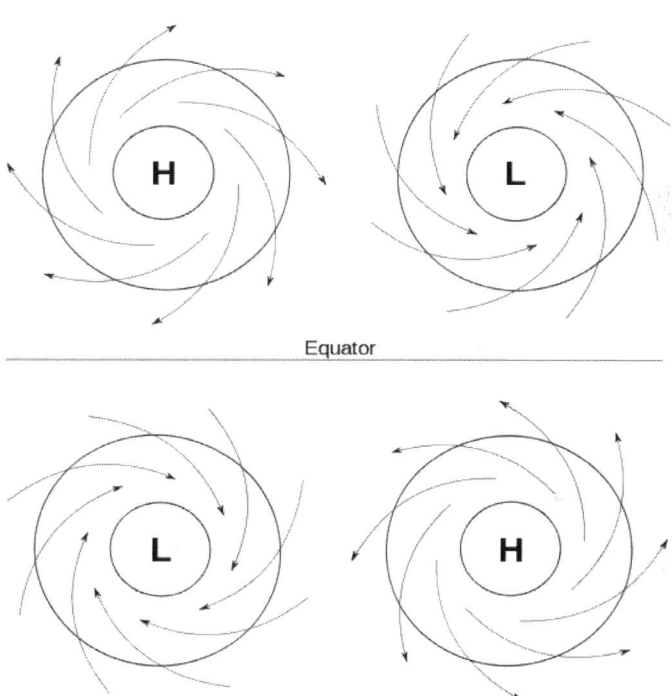

The closer two adjacent isobars are, the steeper the air pressure gradient between them. When isobars are closely spaced it indicates that strong winds exist in the area because air flows rapidly down a steep pressure gradient from areas of high pressure towards areas of low pressure.

In an anticyclone or high pressure system successive isobars are relatively far apart. This results in light winds. In a cyclone or low pressure system, the isobars are more closely spaced. This represents a steeper pressure gradient and the winds are stronger.

Since an anticyclonic area is a region of outflowing winds, air is drawn into it from aloft. This descending air is warmed as it drops toward the earth's surface from higher altitudes. As this air becomes warmer, its capacity for holding uncondensed moisture increases. Therefore, under these conditions, clouds tend to dissipate and clearing skies are characteristic of an anticyclone, although you may still encounter scattered clouds and showers.

In contrast, a cyclonic area is one of converging or inwardly flowing winds. The resulting upward movement of air results in cooling. Since cool air is capable of holding less moisture than warm air, a condition favorable to the formation of clouds and precipitation develops. More or less continuous rain and generally stormy weather is usually associated with a cyclone.

South of the horse latitudes in tropical regions, cyclones only form occasionally over certain areas at sea, and then generally in the summer and fall only. These tropical cyclones are usually quite violent and are known as hurricanes in the Atlantic and typhoons in the Pacific Ocean.

In the areas of the prevailing westerlies in temperate latitudes, a constant procession of cyclones ("lows") and anticyclones ("highs") are a common occurrence. These are sometimes called extratropical cyclones and extratropical anticyclones to distinguish them from the more violent tropical cyclones. The prefix "extra" means "outside of," and in this case refers to weather patterns that are generated outside of the tropics. Formation of these rotating air masses occurs over both sea and land. The lows intensify as they move toward the poles. The highs weaken as they move toward the equator. In their early stages, cyclones are elongated, but as their life cycle proceeds, they become more nearly circular.

Buys Ballot Law

If you wish to determine the location of the center of a low pressure system, determine if you are in the dangerous or navigable semicircle of a cyclone. You will need to know and be able to apply a general rule established by the Dutch meteorologist Buys Ballot in 1857. The Buys Ballot Law can be stated as follows: If you are in the northern hemisphere and face into the surface wind, the center of low pressure is toward your right and somewhat behind you. Under the same conditions the center of high pressure is toward your left and somewhat in front of you and the rotation is reversed south of the equator.

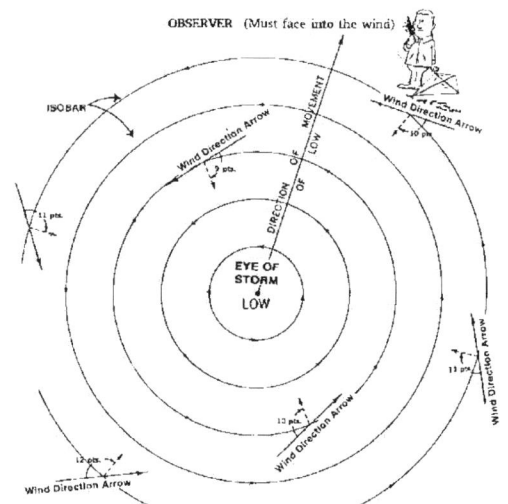

When a cyclone passes north of you in the northern hemisphere, winds shift to the right and are "veering." This indicates that you are in the dangerous semicircle of a cyclone. When a cyclone passes south of you the wind shifts to the left and winds are "backing," which tells you that you are in the navigable semicircle of a cyclone.

Maneuvering to Avoid the Storm Center

The safest procedure with respect to tropical cyclones is to avoid them. If action is taken sufficiently early, this is simply a matter of setting a course that will take the vessel well to one side of the probable track of the storm, and then continuing to plot the positions of the storm center as given in weather bulletins, revising the course as needed.

However, this is not always possible. If the ship is found to be within the storm area the proper action to take depends in part upon its position relative to the storm center and its direction of travel. It is customary to divide the circular area of the storm into two parts.

In the Northern Hemisphere the part to the right of the storm track (facing in the direction toward which the storm is moving) is called the Dangerous Semicircle. It is considered dangerous because (1) the actual wind speed is greater than that due to the pressure gradient alone, since it is augmented by the forward motion of the storm, and (2) the direction of the wind and sea is such as to carry a vessel into the path of the storm (in the forward part of the semicircle).

The part to the left of the storm track is called the less dangerous semicircle or the navigable semicircle. In this part the wind is decreased by the forward motion of the storm and the wind blows vessels away from the storm track (in the forward part). Because of the greater wind speed in the dangerous semicircle, the seas are higher than in the less dangerous semicircle. In the Southern Hemisphere the dangerous semicircle is to the left of the storm track and the less dangerous semicircle is to the right of the storm track.

The wind is perhaps the most reliable guide to indicate in which semicircle the vessel is located. Within the cyclonic circulation, a wind shifting to the right in the northern hemisphere and to the left in the southern hemisphere indicates the vessel is probably in the dangerous semicircle. A steady wind shift opposite this indicates the vessel is probably in the less dangerous semicircle.

As a general rule for a vessel in the Northern Hemisphere, safety lies in placing the wind on the starboard bow in the dangerous semicircle, and on the starboard quarter in the less dangerous semicircle. If on the storm track ahead of the storm, the wind should be put about 160° on the starboard quarter until the vessel is well within the less dangerous semicircle, and the rule for that semicircle should then be followed. In the Southern Hemisphere the same rules hold, but with respect to the port side.

Fronts

A weather front is a boundary separating two air masses of different densities (temperature and moisture), and is the main cause of weather events. Compared to the air masses the fronts are very thin and represented on a weather map using various colored lines and symbols, depending on the type of front. At the frontal surface one air mass is generally overtaking the other and clashing with it. Regardless of which air mass is advancing the warmer less dense air is always forced aloft. Norwegian meteorologists saw these zones of air mass interactions as battlefields and coined the term "fronts." We will be looking at warm fronts, cold fronts, stationary fronts, and occluded fronts.

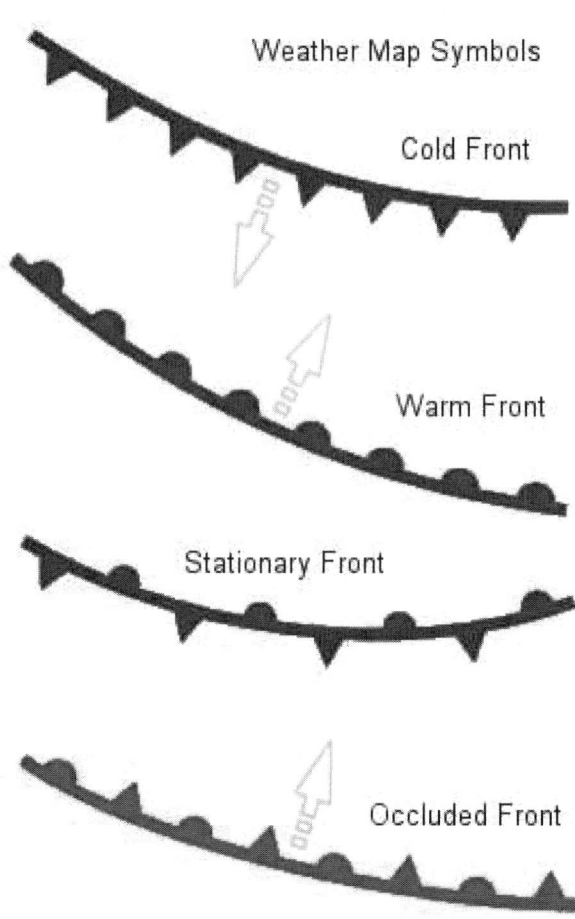

Warm front

When the surface (ground) position of a front moves so that warm air occupies a space formerly occupied by colder air, it is a warm front. On a weather map, a warm front is shown by a red line with red semicircles pointing in the direction of travel. As the cold air retreats, friction with the ground greatly reduces the speed of the surface portion compared to the portion aloft.

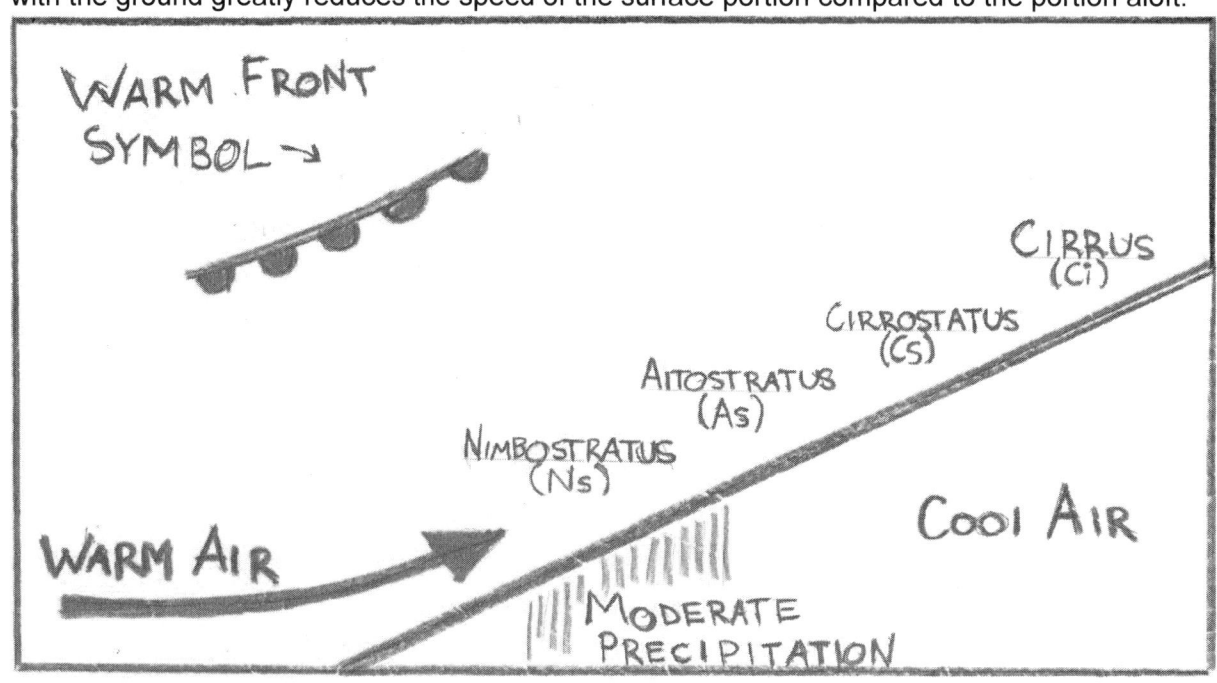

Stated another way the warm, less dense air has a hard time displacing the cold air and the upper part of the warm front ends up way out in front of the surface portion creating a very gradual slope of about 1:150.

As the portion of the front which is aloft is pushed higher over the colder denser air it begins to cool and precipitate moisture in the form of cirrus clouds. While the front draws nearer cirrus clouds give way to cirrostratus, thicken into denser altostratus which eventually gives way to nimbostratus when the front is about 150 miles away, and it starts raining.

The decreasing pressure, indicated by a falling barometer, often indicates the approach of such a wave. In a slow-moving, well-developed warm wave, the barometer may begin to fall several days before the wave arrives. Therefore, the amount and nature of this change in atmospheric pressure between observations assists in predicting the approach of such a system.

As the warm front passes, the temperature raises, the wind shifts in a clockwise direction (i.e. "veers") and the steady rain stops. Drizzle may still continue to fall from low-lying stratus clouds, or there may be fog for some time after the wind shift. During passage of the warm sector between the warm front and the cold front, there is little change in temperature or pressure.

Cold Front

When cold air advances into a region occupied by warmer air the zone of discontinuity is called a cold front. The advancing cold air, being heavier and denser, tends to cut under the warmer air at the leading edge of the cold front and the warmer air is forced aloft. Cold fronts tend be about twice as steep as warm fronts, with a slope of about 1:75 with the portion of the front positioned aloft behind the surface portion. In addition they travel at speeds that average between 20 and 35 mph, compared to a warm front which averages around 15 to 20 mph. The

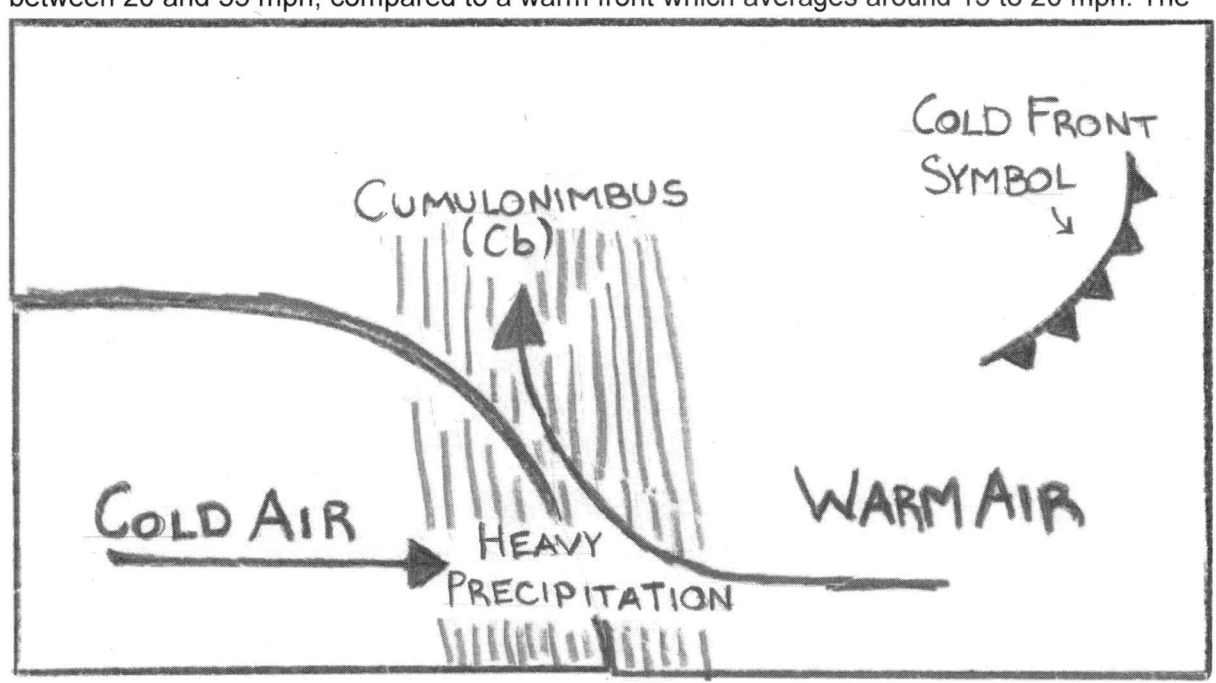

two characteristics of a cold front -being steeper and faster than a warm front -largely account for the more severe nature of the weather that is associated with the passage of cold fronts.

As the faster moving and steeper cold front passes, the wind shifts in a clockwise direction ("veers"), the temperature falls rapidly, and there are often brief and sometimes violent showers, frequently accompanied by thunder and lightning. Clouds are usually of the convective type signifying a vertical movement of air within. A cold front usually coincides with a well-defined wind-shift line along which the wind shifts abruptly from southerly or southwesterly to northerly or northwesterly direction. At sea a series of brief showers accompanied by strong, shifting winds may occur along or at some distance (up to 200 miles) ahead of a cold front. These are called squalls. In common nautical use the term squall may also be applied to any severe local storm accompanied by gusty winds, precipitation, thunder, and lightning. The line along which squalls occur is called a squall line.

Because of its greater speed and steeper slope, a cold front and its associated weather pass more quickly than a warm front. After a cold front passes, the pressure rises, often quite rapidly, the visibility usually improves, and the clouds tend to diminish. On a weather map cold fronts are represented by blue lines with blue triangles pointing in the direction of travel.

Occluded Front

An occluded front occurs when a cold front overtakes a warm front around mature low-pressure areas. The warm air has been forced upwards and there are now two cool air masses adjacent to each other. When the two parts of the cold air mass meet, the warmer portion tends to rise above the colder part. The warm air continues to rise until the entire frontal system dissipates (i.e. breaks down). As the warmer air is replaced by colder air, the pressure gradually increases, a process called "filling". This

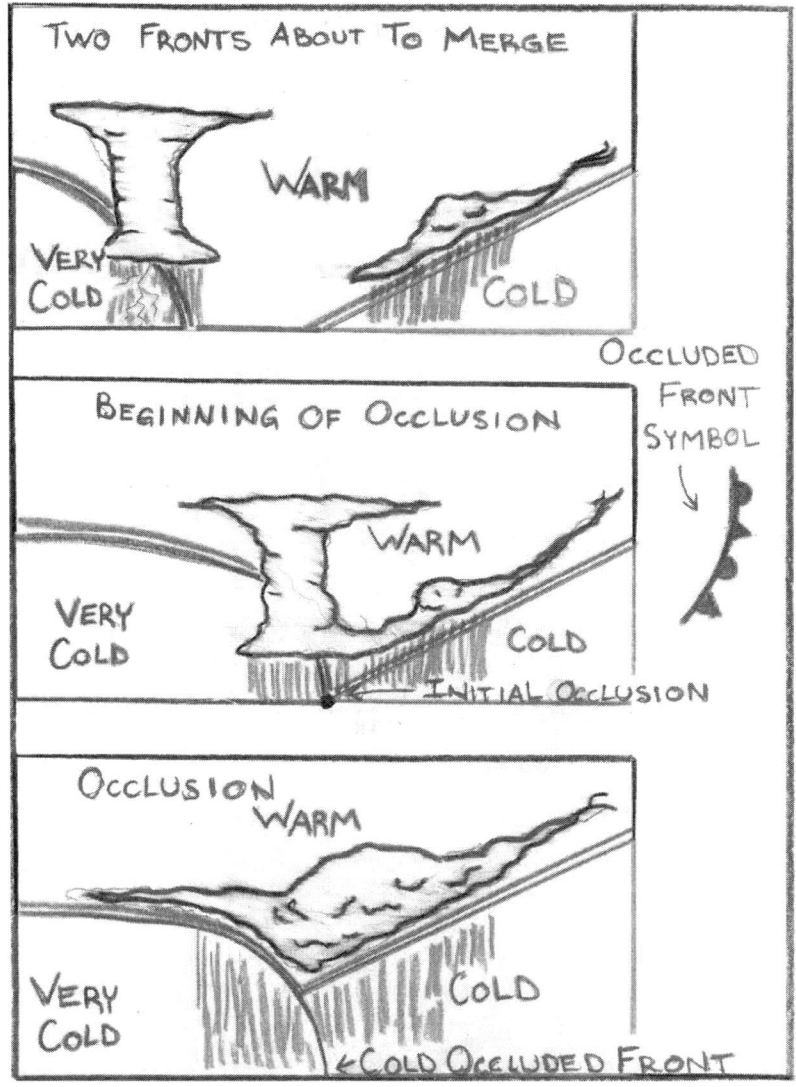

usually occurs within a few days after an occluded front forms. Finally, a low pressure system with little or no gradient in temperature is formed.

Stationary Front

At times the airflow on both sides of a front is neither toward the cold air mass nor toward the warm air mass, but almost parallel to the line of the front. Consequently, the surface portion of the front does not move, or moves very slowly. This condition is called a stationary front. On a weather map, stationary fronts are shown with blue triangular points on one side of the line and red semicircles on the other. Because warm air is usually gliding up against cool air along stationary fronts, gentle to moderate precipitation is likely. Stationary fronts may stay over an area for several days and produce rain which may cause flooding.

Clouds

Clouds are visible collections of numerous tiny droplets of water, or ice crystals, formed by the condensation of water vapor in the air. The base (bottom) of a cloud is generally above the surface of the earth. Fog is similar to a cloud, but its base or bottom layer is in actual contact with the earth's surface.

The shape, size, height, thickness and nature of a cloud depend upon the conditions under which it is formed. Therefore, clouds serve as visible indicators of the various processes that are continually taking place in the atmosphere. The ability to recognize different types of clouds and knowledge of the conditions that are associated with them is useful in predicting and forecasting future weather.

Although the variety of clouds is virtually endless, they may be classified according to their general types. Clouds are grouped generally into three families according to their most common characteristics.

High clouds are those whose mean lower level is above 18,000 feet and whose tops may reach to 40,000 feet or more. Because of their height, these clouds are composed principally of ice crystals. Middle clouds are found between 6,000 and about 18,000 feet. They are composed largely of water droplets, although the higher ones have a tendency toward ice particles. Low clouds have a mean lower level of less than 6,000 feet. These clouds are composed of water droplets.

Within these 3 families are ten principal cloud types. The names of these cloud types are composed of various combinations and forms of the following basic words, all taken from Latin. Remembering these words will make the job of learning about them much easier.
- Cirrus means "curl, lock, or tuft of hair"
- Cumulus means "a heap, pile, or an accumulation"
- Stratus means "spread out, flattened, or covered with a layer"

- Alto means "high or upper air"
- Nimbus means "rainy cloud"

Individual cloud types are recognized by certain characteristics, variations, or combinations of these. There are ten principal cloud types.

The illustration below is the one used on exams. The cloud types above are numbered according the the diagram. Stratus clouds are not on the diagram hence nine cloud types and not ten. Be sure to understand all of the nine cloud types indicated on it as described in the following paragraphs.

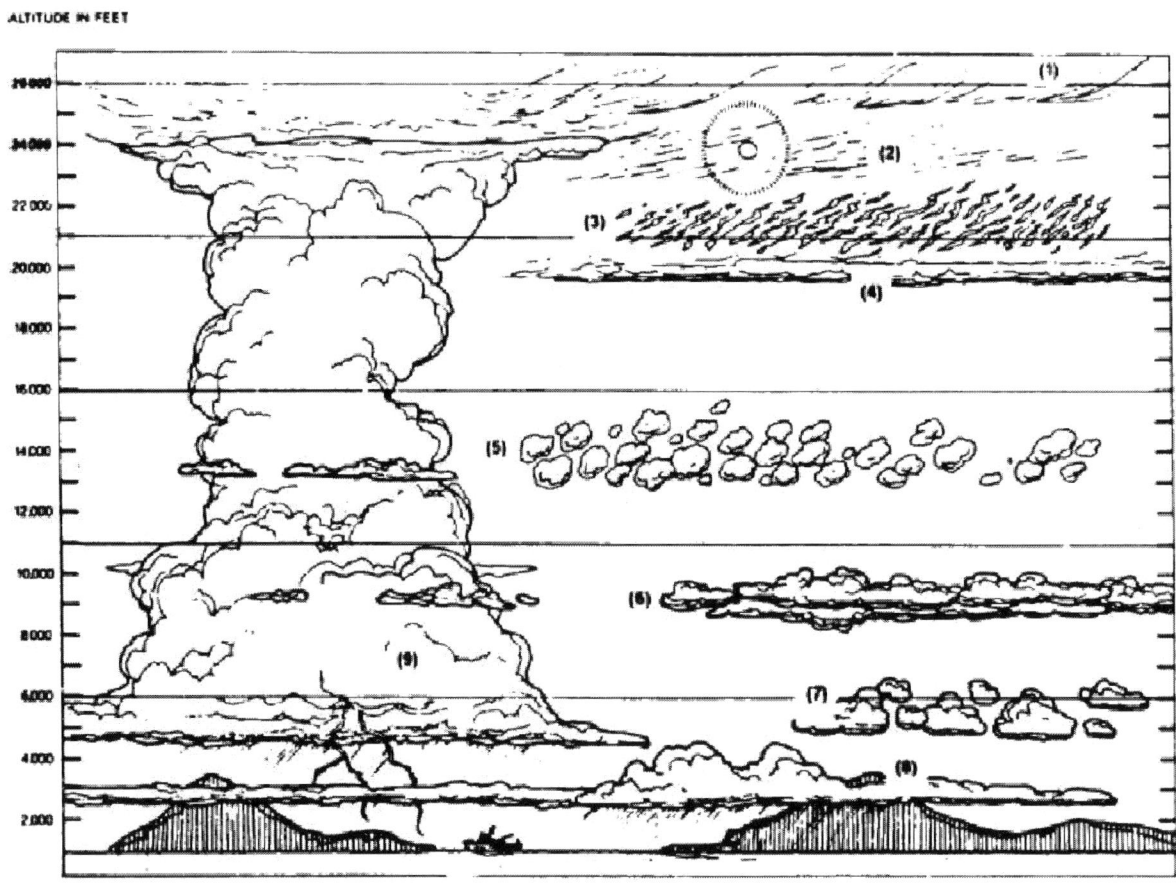

High Clouds

1. Cirrus Clouds

Cirrus clouds are detached high clouds of delicate and fibrous appearance, without darkness or shading, generally white in color, and often silky in appearance. Their fibrous and feathery appearance results from the fact that they are composed entirely of ice crystals. Cirrus clouds appear in varied forms such as isolated tufts, which are long, thin lines across the sky, branching, feather-like plumes, or curved wisps which may end in tufts, etc. These clouds may be arranged in parallel bands which cross the sky in great circles and appear to converge or come together toward a point on the horizon. This may indicate, in a very general way, the approximate direction of a low pressure area. Cirrus clouds may be brilliantly colored at sunrise and sunset. Because of their height, they become illuminated by the sun's rays before other clouds in the morning, and remain lighted after others at sunset. Cirrus clouds are generally associated with fair weather. However, if cirrus clouds are followed by lower and thicker clouds, they are often the forerunners of rain or snow.

2. Cirrostratus Clouds

Cirrostratus clouds are thin, whitish, high clouds that sometimes cover the sky completely and give it a milky appearance. At other times cirrostratus clouds present, more or less distinctly, a formation like a tangled web. The thin veil of cirrostratus clouds is not sufficiently dense to blur the outline of the sun or moon. However, the ice crystals that compose these clouds refract (i.e. bend the rays of...) the light passing through in such a way that halos may form with either the sun or moon at the center. Cirrus clouds frequently thicken and change into cirrostratus ones. In this form the cloud is popularly known as "mares' tails." If the clouds continue to thicken and lower, the ice crystals may melt to form water droplets, and the cloud formation becomes known as altostratus. When this occurs, rain can normally be expected to arrive within 24 hours. Evidence of stronger winds at the level of the clouds may be seen if the cirrus clouds become more brush like.

3. Cirrocumulus Clouds

Cirrocumulus clouds are high and composed of small white flakes or scales, or of very small globular masses. Usually they appear without shadows and are arranged in groups or lines, or more often in ripples resembling those of sand on the seashore. One form of cirrocumulus clouds is popularly known as a "mackerel sky" because the pattern resembles the scales on the back of a mackerel. Like cirrus, cirrocumulus clouds are composed of ice crystals and are generally associated with fair weather, but may precede a storm if they thicken and lower. They may turn gray and appear to harden before thickening.

Middle Clouds

4. Altostratus Clouds

Altostratus clouds are middle clouds with a grayish or bluish appearance in a fibrous veil or sheet. The sun or moon, when seen through these clouds, appears as if it were shining through ground glass, with a corona or a glow of light around it. However, no halo is formed. If these clouds thicken and lower, or if low, ragged "scud" or rain clouds (nimbostratus) form below them, continuous rain or snow may be expected within a few hours.

5. Altocumulus Clouds

Altocumulus clouds are middle clouds that consist of a layer of large, ball like masses that tend to merge together. The balls or patches may vary in thickness and color from dazzling white to dark gray, but they are arranged in a more or less regular pattern. They may appear as distinct patches or similar to cirrocumulus clouds, however, altocumulus clouds can be distinguished by the way that individual patches are generally larger, and show distinct shadows in some places. They are often mistaken for stratocumulus clouds. If this cloud formation thickens and lowers, it may produce thundery weather and showers, but it does not bring prolonged bad weather. Sometimes the patches merge to form a series of big rolls that resemble ocean waves, but with intermittent streaks of blue sky. Because of your perspective (i.e. the way the clouds appear from where you are standing), the rolls appear to run together near the horizon. These regular parallel bands differ from cirrocumulus clouds in that they occur in larger masses with shadows. These clouds move in the direction of the short dimension of the rolls, as do ocean waves. They are generally arranged in a line with a flat horizontal base, giving the impression of turrets on a castle. The turreted tops may look like miniature cumulus clouds and possess considerable depth and great length. These clouds usually indicate a change to chaotic, thundery skies.

Low Clouds

6. Stratocumulus Clouds

Stratocumulus clouds are low clouds composed of soft, gray, roll-shaped masses. They may be shaped in long, parallel rolls similar to altocumulus clouds that are moving forward with the wind. The motion is in the direction of their short dimension, like ocean waves. These clouds, which vary greatly in altitude, are the final product of the characteristic daily change that takes place in cumulus clouds. They are usually followed by clear skies during the night.

7. Cumulus Clouds

Cumulus clouds are dense clouds with pronounced vertical development These clouds are formed by rising air which is cooled as it reaches greater heights- Cumulus clouds have horizontal bases and dome-shaped upper surfaces, with protuberances (i.e. bulges or swellings) that extend above the dome. Cumulus clouds appear in small patches, and never cover the entire sky. When the vertical development is not great, the clouds appear in patches resembling tufts of cotton or wool and are popularly called "woolpack" clouds. The horizontal bases of these clouds may not be noticeable because they are cut off by the horizon. These are called "fair weather" cumulus, because they always accompany good weather. However, they may merge with altocumulus, or may grow to cumulonimbus before a thunderstorm. Since cumulus clouds are formed by updrafts, they are accompanied by turbulence or a churning motion that causes "bumpiness" in the air which is noticeable in aircraft. The extent of this turbulence is proportional to the vertical extent of the clouds. Cumulus clouds are marked by strong contrasts of light and darkness.

8. Nimbostratus Clouds

Nimbostratus clouds are a low, dark, shapeless cloud layer, usually uniform or nearly so, but sometimes with ragged, wet-looking bases. Nimbostratus is the typical rain cloud. The precipitation which falls from this cloud may be steady or intermittent, but it cannot be classified as showery.

9. Cumulonimbus Clouds

Cumulonimbus clouds are massive clouds with great vertical development that rise in mountainous towers to great heights. The upper part of the cloud consists of ice crystals, and often spreads out in the shape of an anvil. The anvil top is a characteristic of this type of cloud. Cumulonimbus clouds may be seen at great distances because of their great height but their bases may not be visible because they are below the horizon. Cumulonimbus clouds often produce showers of rain, snow, or hail, frequently accompanied by thunder. Because of this, the cumulonimbus cloud is often popularly called a "thundercloud" or "thunderhead". The base is horizontal, but as showers occur it lowers and becomes ragged.

10. Stratus Clouds

Stratus is a low cloud in a uniform layer resembling fog. Often the base of the cloud is no more than 1,000 feet high. A veil of thin stratus gives the sky a hazy appearance. However, stratus clouds are often quite thick, and permit so little sunlight to pass through that it appears dark to an observer below. From above, these clouds look white, and alight mist may descend from a layer of stratus clouds. On occasion a strong wind may break stratus into shreds called "fractostratus" (i.e. fractured or broken). Note that the Stratus cloud is not identified in the exam diagram.

Fog

Fog is really a cloud whose base touches the surface of the earth and causes restricted visibility. Fog is composed of droplets of water (or, under certain conditions, ice crystals called ice fog), and is formed by condensation or crystallization of water vapor in the air. There are several different types of fog as discussed below.

Radiation fog

Radiation fog forms over low-lying land on clear, calm nights. As the land radiates heat and becomes cooler, it cools the air immediately above the surface. This causes a temperature inversion to form. In a temperature inversion the temperature for some distance upward increases with height. This is somewhat abnormal and unusual. Fog forms when the air just above the earth's surface is cooled below its dew point by the cooled land. Often, cooler and more dense air drains down surrounding slopes to heighten this effect. Radiation fog is often quite shallow and is usually most dense at the surface. After sunrise this type of fog may "lift" and gradually dissipate so that it is usually gone by noon. At sea the temperature of the water undergoes little change between day and night. Consequently, radiation fog is seldom encountered more than 10 miles offshore.

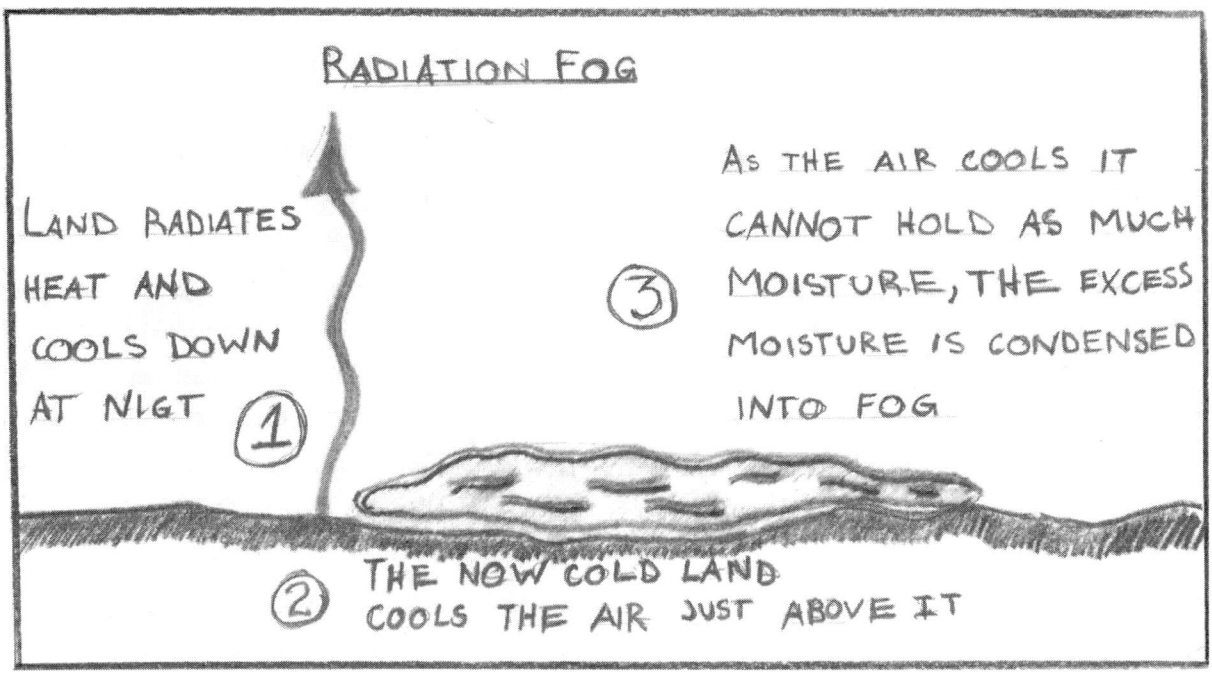

Advection fog

Advection fog forms when warm, moist air blows over a colder surface and is cooled below its dew point. This type of fog, most commonly encountered at sea, may be quite dense and often persists over relatively long periods. In other words, do not expect morning fog to be gone by noon. Advection fog is common over cold ocean currents. If the wind is strong enough to thoroughly mix the air, condensation may take place at some distance above the surface of the earth, and form low stratus clouds rather than fog.

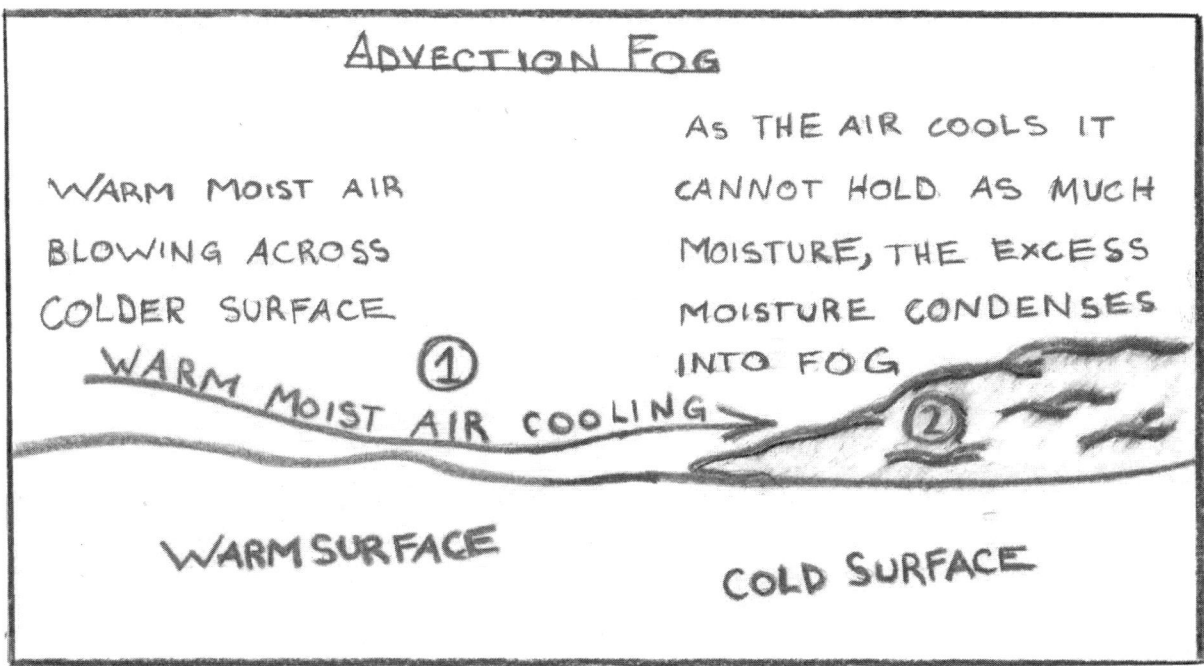

Sea Smoke

When very cold air moves over warmer water, wisps of visible water vapor may rise from the surface as the water "steams". In extreme cases this frost smoke, or arctic sea smoke, may rise to a height of several hundred feet. The portion near the surface becomes a dense fog which obscures the horizon and objects on the surface of the water, but usually leaves the sky relatively clear.

Haze

Haze consists of fine dust or small particles in the air, too small to be individually apparent, but in sufficient numbers reduces horizontal visibility and cast a bluish or yellowish veil over the landscape, subduing its colors and making objects appear indistinct. This is sometimes called dry haze to distinguish it from damp haze, which consists of small water droplets or moist particles in the air that are smaller and more scattered than light fog. Consequently, the term "haze" refers to a condition of atmospheric obscurity caused by dust and smoke.

Compass - Magnetic and Gyro

Compass

The principle of the present day magnetic compass is no different from that of the compasses used by ancient mariners. The magnetic compass consists of a magnetized needle allowed to rotate in the horizontal plane. The superiority of present day magnetic compasses over ancient ones results from a better knowledge of the laws of magnetism, which govern the behavior of the compass, and from greater precision in design and construction.

Any magnetized piece of metal will have regions of concentrated magnetism called poles. Any such magnet will have at least two poles of opposite polarity. Magnetic force (flux) lines connect one pole of such a magnet with the other pole. The number of such lines per unit area represents the intensity of the magnetic field in that area. If two magnets are placed close to each other, the like poles will repel each other and the unlike poles will attract each other.

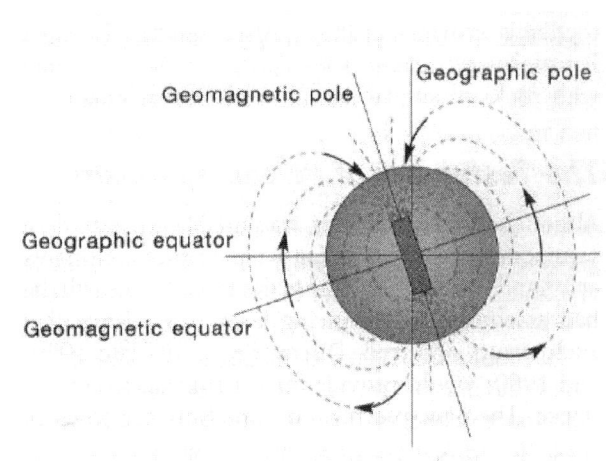

Terrestrial Magnetism

Consider the Earth as a huge magnet surrounded by lines of magnetic flux connecting its two magnetic poles. These magnetic poles are near, but not coincidental with, the Earth's geographic poles as shown in the figure on the right.

Variation

Since the magnetic poles of the Earth do not coincide with the geographic poles, a compass needle in line with the Earth's magnetic field will not indicate true north, but magnetic north. The angular difference between the True North (great circle connecting the geographic poles) and the Magnetic North (direction of the lines of magnetic flux) is called variation. This variation has different values at different locations on the Earth. These values of magnetic variation may be found on pilot charts and on the compass rose of navigational charts.

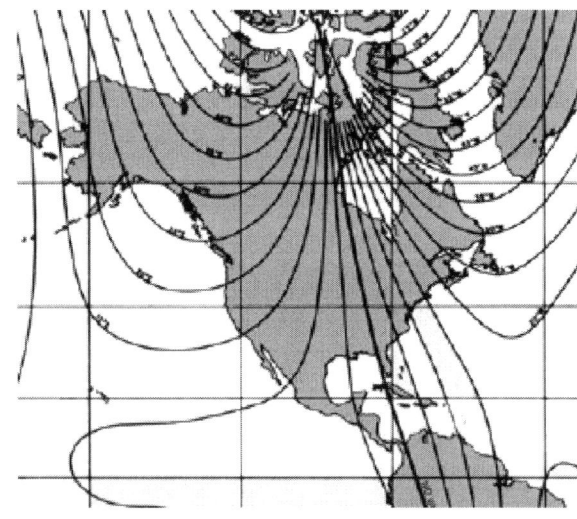

The poles are not geographically static; they are known to migrate slowly. Therefore the variation for most areas undergoes a small annual change, the amount of which is also noted on charts. The Figure at right above shows a graphical representation of the variation for North America. Notice that the variation is small in the Great Lakes area and much larger on the east and west coasts. The variation can be either West or East. Up-to-date information on geomagnetics is available at http://geomag.usgs.gov.

Ship's Magnetism

A ship under construction or repair will acquire permanent magnetism due to hammering and vibration while sitting stationary in the Earth's magnetic field. After launching, the ship will lose some of this original magnetism as a result of vibration and pounding in varying magnetic fields, and will eventually reach a more or less stable magnetic condition. The magnetism which remains is the permanent magnetism of the ship.

In addition to its permanent magnetism, a ship acquires induced magnetism when placed in the Earth's magnetic field. The magnetism induced in any given piece of soft iron is a function of the field intensity, the alignment of the soft iron in that field, and the physical properties and dimensions of the iron. This induced magnetism may add to - or subtract from - the permanent magnetism already present in the ship, depending on how the ship is aligned in the magnetic field. The softer the iron, the more readily it will be magnetized by the Earth's magnetic field, and the more readily it will give up its magnetism when removed from that field.

Deviation

The magnetism in the various structures of a ship, which tends to change as a result of cruising, vibration, or aging is called sub-permanent magnetism. This magnetism, at any instant, is part of the ship's permanent magnetism, and consequently must be corrected by permanent magnet correctors. It is the principal cause of the deviation on a magnetic compass. Subsequent reference to permanent magnetism will refer to the apparent permanent magnetism which includes the existing permanent and sub permanent magnetism.

A ship, then, has a combination of permanent, sub permanent, and induced magnetism. Therefore, the ship's apparent permanent magnetic condition is subject to change. The ship's induced magnetism will vary with the Earth's magnetic field strength and with the alignment of the ship in that field or more clearly, the heading of the ship.

Most compasses can have a "Magnetic Adjustment." This can minimize the deviation of the Ship's Compass Magnetism but not totally eliminate it. To allow us to correct for this deviation in the compass, Deviation Tables are established for each ship. The deviation table is unique to each ship and gives the deviation for a series of headings. It is very important to remember that the deviation depends on the heading of the ship. A favorite trap in range and deviation chart navigation questions is to imply that the deviation is dependent on the bearing of an object. Deviation is dependent only on the heading of the vessel.

On the Coast Guard exam covering charting, all of the compass values used on the chart are in degrees TRUE. When you look at your compass to check your course or heading, or to take a bearing, the value you read is not in true but in PSC. There are several phrases used to describe this reading. The most common are:

- Per Steering Compass
- Per Standard Magnetic Compass
- Per Standard Compass
- PSC

Notice that they all have the word <u>compass</u> in them. It is important that you remember that all of your work on the exams will be between COMPASS and TRUE. To get from COMPASS to TRUE you have two corrections to make. First you must correct for the ship itself (deviation), then you must correct for the difference between the earth's magnetic poles and geographic poles (variation).

Magnetic is only the middle step in the correction process. It is <u>never</u> put on the chart. It is <u>never</u> given in a problem. It is <u>never</u> an answer.

Navigation and Position Determination

Charts

Latitude, Longitude and the Compass Rose

Latitude is on the vertical axis or sides of the chart and used to measure distance. Longitude is on the horizontal axis or top and bottom of the chart and specifies East - West position of a point on a chart. The outer ring of a compass rose on a nautical chart provides true directions. The inner ring of a compass rose on a nautical chart provides magnetic directions.

Mercator projection

Navigators most often use the plane conformal projection known as the Mercator projection. The Mercator projection is not perspective, and its parallels can be derived mathematically as well as projected geometrically. Its distinguishing feature is that both the meridians (Longitude) and parallels (Latitude) are expanded at the same ratio with increased latitude. What does this mean? When you look at the chart the Longitude lines are all parallel to each other and cross Latitude lines at a 90° angle. Since the projection is conformal, expansion is the same in all directions and angles are correctly shown. Rhumb lines appear as straight lines, the directions of which can be measured directly on the chart. Distances can also be measured directly if the spread of latitude is small. Great circles, except meridians and the equator, appear as curved lines concave to the equator. Small areas appear in their correct shape but of increased size unless they are near the equator.

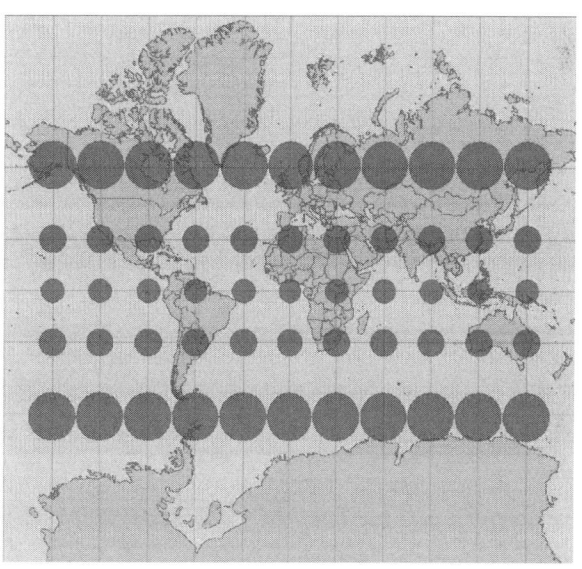

Definition: 1 minute of latitude = 1 nautical mile

Proof:

$$\frac{21{,}642 \; nauticle \; miles}{1 \; earth \; circumference} \times \frac{1 \; earth \; circumfrance}{360 \; degrees} \times \frac{1 \; degree}{60 \; minutes} = \frac{1 \; nauticle \; mile}{1 \; minute}$$

On a Mercator chart the scale varies with the latitude. This is noticeable on a chart covering a relatively large distance in a north-south direction. On such a chart the border scale near the latitude in question should be used for measuring distances.

Aids to Navigation

Lateral Aids

Starboard Side

Use the the acronym **RENT** to remember everything you need to know about starboard marks.
- R - They are **Red**
- E - They have **Even** numbers
- N - Unlighted buoys are called **Nuns**
- T - The shape associated with them is a **Triangle**

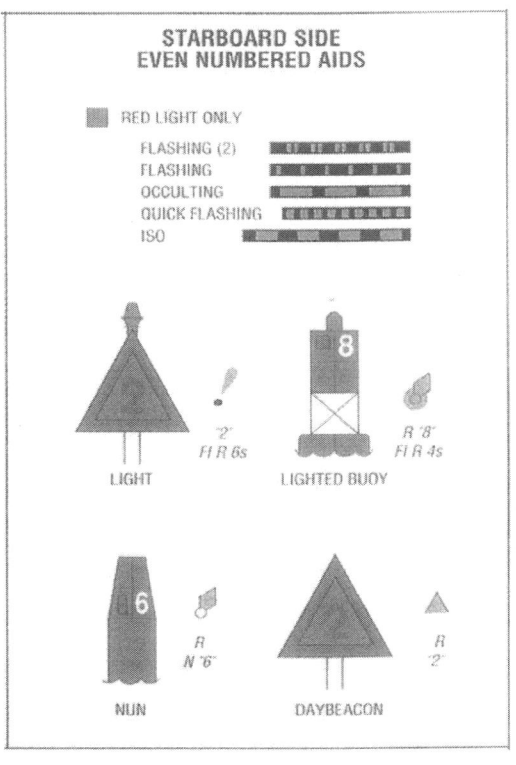

Port Side

Use the the acronym **COGS** to remember everything you need to know about starboard marks.
- C - Unlighted buoys are called **Cans**
- O - They have **Odd** numbers
- G - They are **Green**
- S - The shape associated with them is a **Square**

Remember to use the **RENT COGS** acronym to answer questions about starboard and port side

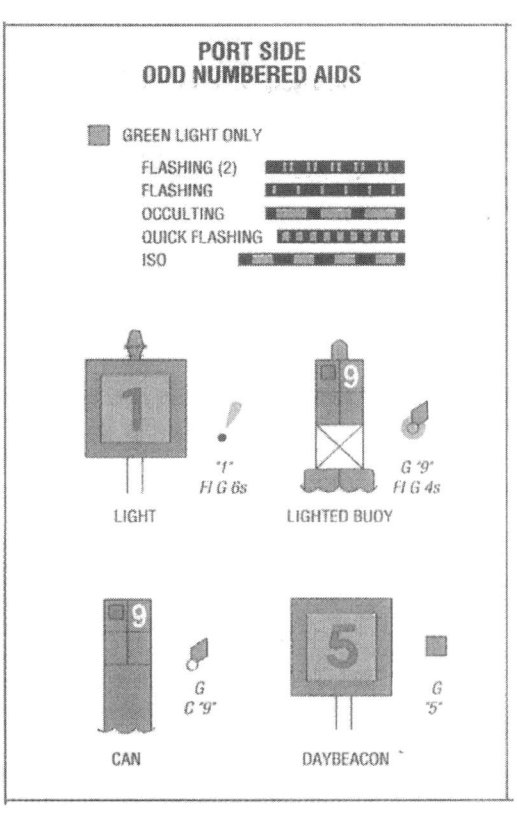

lateral aids to navigation. This same acronym can be used with preferred channel marks.

Preferred Channel

Unlighted, red and green, horizontally-banded buoys with the topmost band red are conical in shape and called nun buoys. Unlighted, green and red, horizontally-banded buoys with the topmost band green are cylindrical in shape and called can buoys. A preferred-channel buoy may be lettered. A preferred-channel buoy may show a red or green light. A preferred-channel buoy will show a light characteristic of composite group-flashing (2 + 1) red or green light.

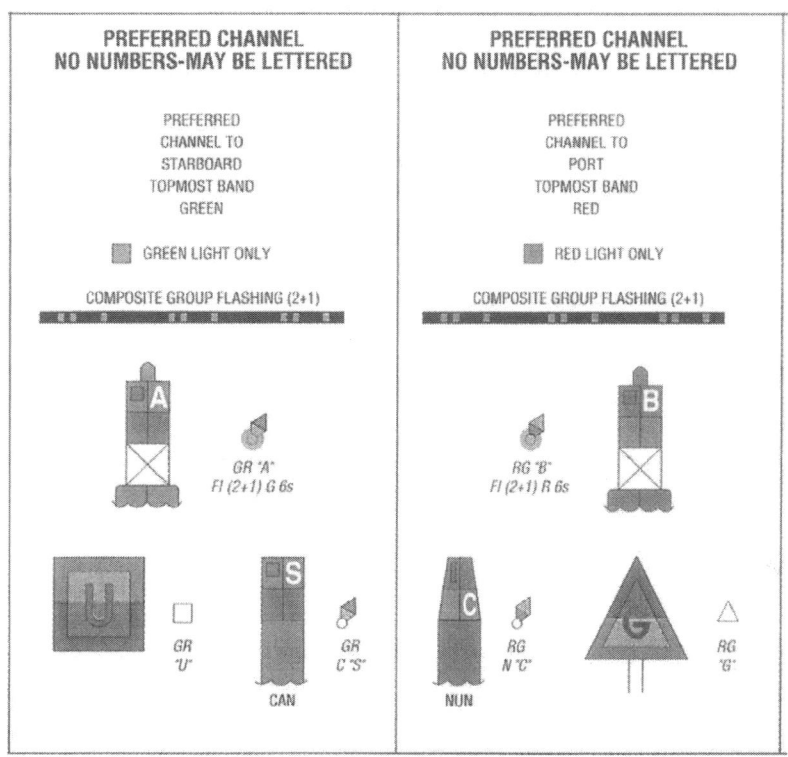

Non Lateral Aids

Isolated Danger

Buoys which mark isolated dangers are painted with alternating red and black bands. Buoys which mark isolated dangers have a light characteristic of Fl (2) Group flashing. Buoys which mark isolated dangers have a white light if lighted. Buoys which mark isolated dangers have a shape on top consisting of two balls. Buoys which mark isolated dangers may be Lettered.

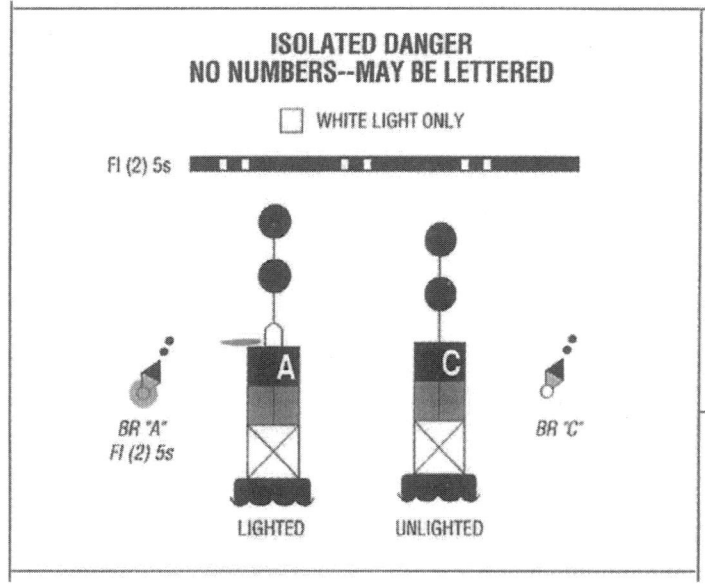

Safe Water

A safe water mark can be passed close aboard on either side. A lighted safe water mark is painted with red and white vertical stripes and has a white Morse (A) light characteristic. A safe water daymark has octagonal shape. A lighted safe water mark fitted with a spherical topmark to aid in its identification. Buoys which mark safe water may be lettered.

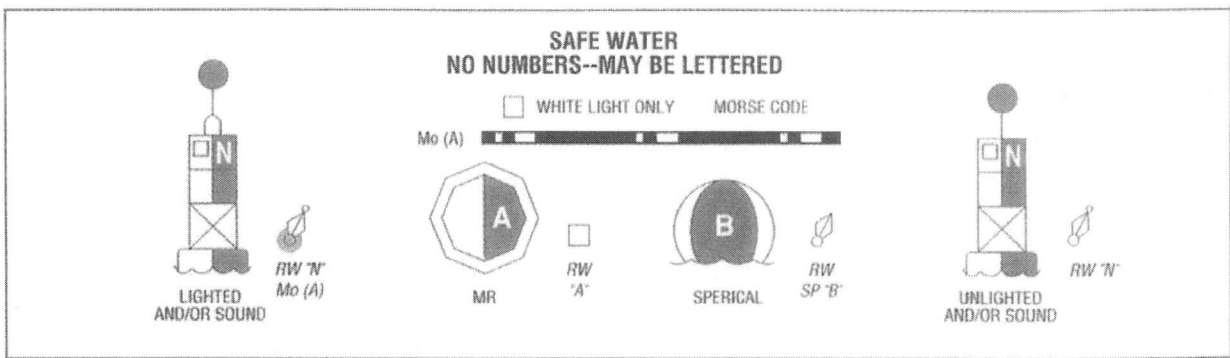

Special Marks

Special mark buoys are yellow and may be nuns or cans. Special mark buoys may be lettered. Lighted special mark buoys show a yellow light. Special mark buoys must show a light characteristic of fixed or flashing yellow light.

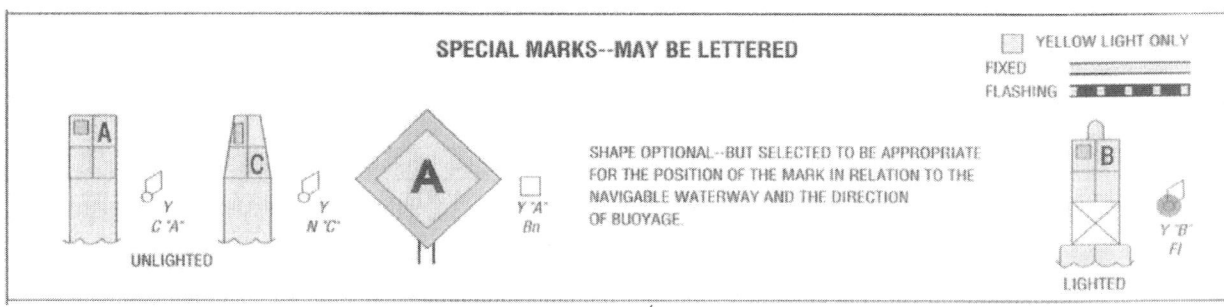

Information and Regulatory Marks

White and orange information and regulatory marks may indicate exclusion area, restricted operations and danger. Lighted white and orange information and regulatory marks have a white light. Lighted information and regulatory marks may display any light characteristic except quick flashing and flashing (2). A white buoy with an orange square on it is an informational and regulatory buoy.

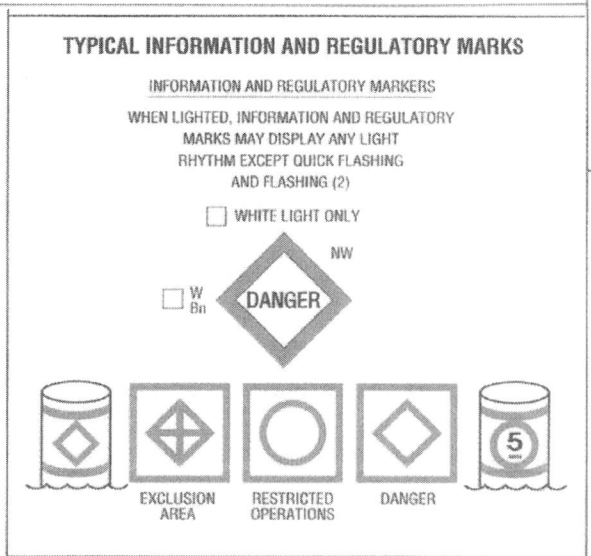

77

Ranges

When you are steering on a pair of range lights and find the upper light is above the lower light, you should continue on the present course. If you are steering on a channel marked by a range. The range is in sight and appears as shown in diagram DO47NG. You should alter course to port and bring the range in line. If you are steering on a channel marked by a range. The range is in sight and appears as shown in diagram DO48NG. You should alter course to starboard and bring the range in line.

DO47NG

DO48NG

Bridges

A swing bridge is open for river traffic at night when the red light changes to green. If you are approaching an open drawbridge and sound the proper signal and you receive no acknowledgment from the bridge, you should approach with caution and proceed through the open draw. A drawbridge may use visual signals to acknowledge a vessel's request to open the draw. The signal which indicates that the draw will NOT be opened immediately is a fixed red light.

If you are approaching a drawbridge and have sounded the proper whistle signal requesting it to open and you hear a signal of one prolonged and one short blast from the bridge, you should approach under full control to pass through the bridge.

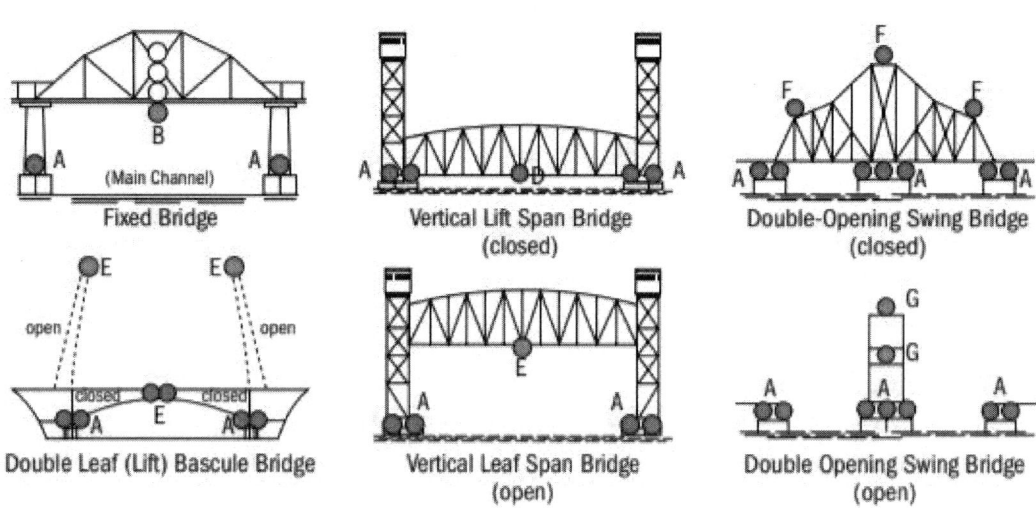

A ● - Piers and supports.

B ● - Centerline of navigable channel.

C ○ - Three white lights stacked vertically show the preferred route, if there is more than one navigable channel.

D ● - Used on some lift bridges to indicate the lift is closed.

E ● - Lift is open to vessel traffic.

F ● - Double-opening swing bridges show three red lights when closed.

G ● - Double-opening swing bridges show two green lights when open.

Light Characteristics

In the U.S. Aids to Navigation System, lateral aids as seen entering from seaward may display lights with these characteristics: flashing, occulting and quick flashing. A light that has a light period shorter than its dark period is described as flashing. An occulting light is one in which the period of light exceeds the period of darkness. An isophase light is one in which the periods of light and darkness are equal. A lighted buoy with a fixed light is one in which the light shows continuously and steady. The period of a lighted aid to navigation refers to the time required for the light to complete each cycle. An alternating light shows a light that changes color.

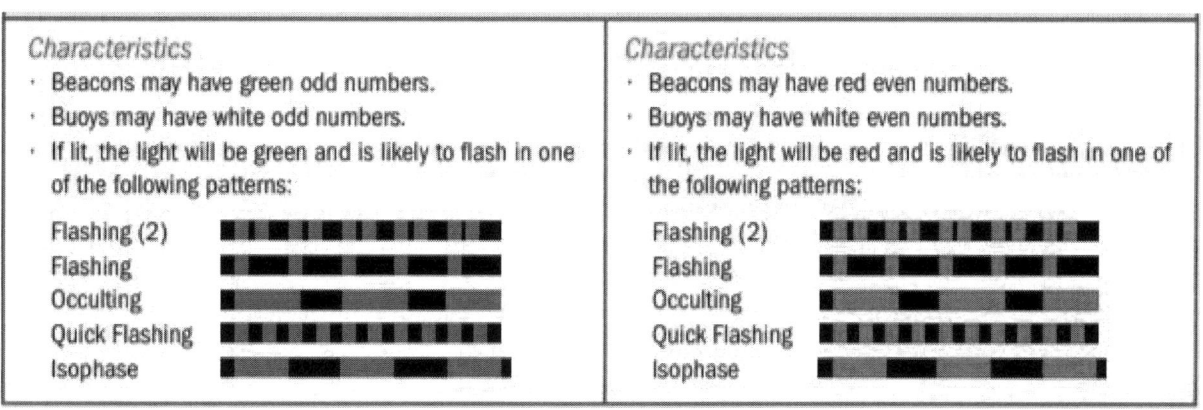

Publications

Light List

A Light List is a detailed list of navigational aids including lighthouses and other lighted navigation aids, unlighted buoys, radiobeacons, daybeacons, and racons.

Coast Pilots

The National Ocean Service Coast Pilot is a series of nine nautical books that cover a wide variety of information important to navigators of U.S. coastal and intracoastal waters, and the waters of the Great Lakes. The information in a Coast Pilot cannot be shown graphically on the standard nautical charts and is not readily available elsewhere.

Coast Pilot contains descriptions of the coast line, buoyage systems, weather conditions, port facilities, and navigation instructions. It also provides information about channel depths, dangers, obstructions, anchorages, and marine facilities available in that port.

Coast Pilot contains information on navigation regulations, landmarks, channels, anchorages, tides, currents, and clearances of bridges for Chesapeake Bay. It would describe the explosive anchorages in the ports on the east coast of the United States.

Tide Tables and Tide Current Tables

Tide Table are used to predict tides including the time and height of a tides at a certain location at any time.

Tide Current Table are used to predict tide currents including the set and drift of a current at a certain location at any time.

Notice to Mariners

Notice to Mariners advises mariners of important matters affecting navigational safety, including new hydrographic information, changes in channels, aids to navigation, and other important data.

Tides and Tidal Currents

Tides and Tidal Currents

Tide is the vertical rise and fall of the water caused by the gravitational "pull" of the moon and sun on different parts of the earth as it rotates through space. As the tide rises and falls it is accompanied by a horizontal movement of the water called tidal current.

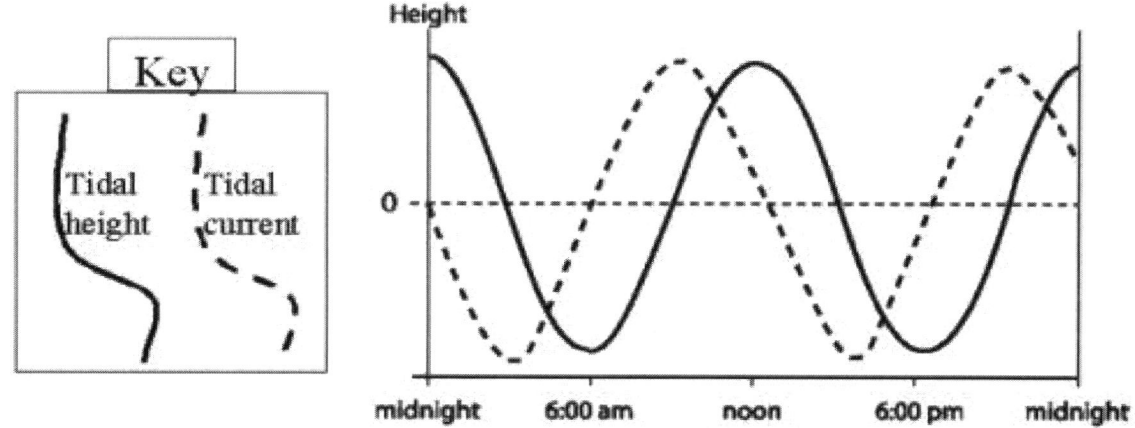

Height of the tide refers to the amount of water in feet above or below the selected tidal datum. For example, if the selected datum is Mean Lower Low Water (MLLW) and the Tide Tables show the height of the tide as +2.0 feet at that time and place, then the height of the tide is 2.0 feet above the chart datum of Mean Lower Low Water.

To obtain the true depth of the water at any point you must first examine a chart of the area and find the sounding that indicates the depth of water at mean lower low water. Then add 2.0 feet to this charted depth to obtain the total depth of the water. Remember that other factors and conditions like storms and winds may affect the actual depth of the water, too. These factors, unlike the tides, are not "predictable."

In many, but not all, parts of the world high tides and low tides each occur twice daily. The tide rises until it reaches a maximum height called "high tide" or high water. Then it falls until it reaches a minimum height called "low tide" or low water.

The tide does not rise and fall at a uniform rate. From low water the tide begins to rise slowly, increasing its rate of rise until it is about halfway to high water. Then the rate of rise begins to slow until high water is reached and the rise ceases. The falling tide acts in the same manner. The tide falls slowly at first, and then at an increasing rate until about halfway to low water. Then the rate of fall decreases until low water when the fall ceases. Consequently, the maximum rate of tide rise or fall is in the area of the half-tide.

The period at high or low water, when there is no noticeable rise or fall of the tide, is called the stand. The vertical distance from low water to high water is the range of that specific tide, often called tidal range.

There are three distinct types of tides and they are; Semidiurnal, Diurnal, and a Mixed tide.

Semidiurnal Tide

Semidiurnal tide has two high waters and two low waters every tidal day (24 hr 50 min). There is relatively little difference between the heights of the two high tides and there is relatively little difference between the heights of the two low waters. Tides on the east coast of the United States are examples of semidiurnal tides. On the

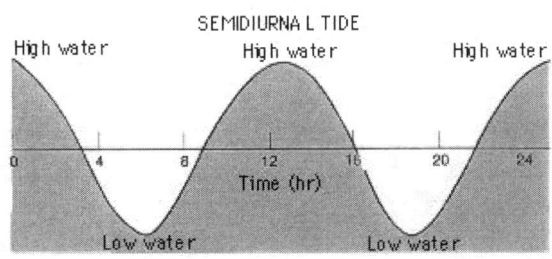

U.S., west coast, and other parts of the world, semidiurnal tides may show a large difference between the two high water heights, the two low water heights, or both.

Diurnal Tide

Diurnal tide has only one high water and one low water each tidal day. This type of tide occurs along parts of the northern shore of the Gulf of Mexico, in the Java Sea, the Gulf of Tonkin, and in a few other areas.

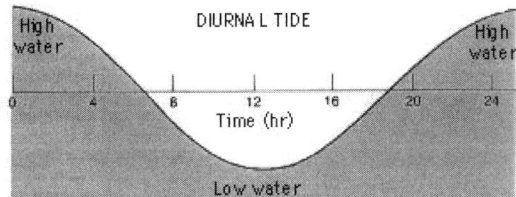

Mixed Tides

Mixed tides have a semidiurnal tidal period but, for a few days of each tidal month, will change to a diurnal period. The diurnal inequality is a characteristic of this tide where successive high tides and/or successive low tides will have significantly different heights each tidal day. The figure below shows an example of a mixed tide.
The graph below shows a mixed tide.

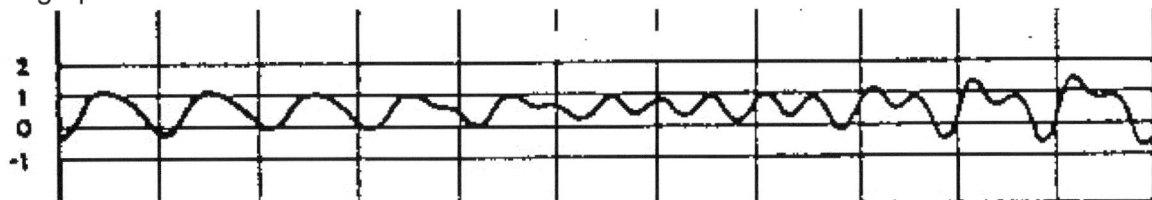

Spring Tides

Spring tides occur when the moon and sun are in line with each other (i.e., either in opposition or conjunction). Spring tides are semidiurnal tides that occur when both celestial bodies the moon and sun are in line with each other so that both exert a gravitational pull together

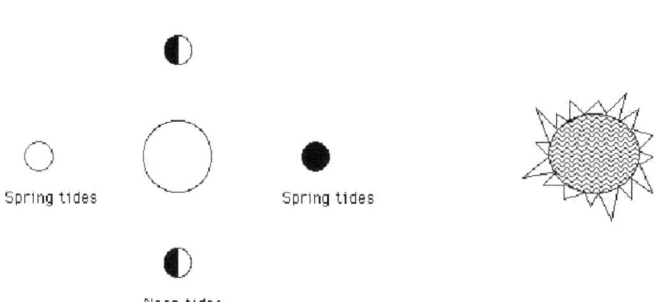

on the earth's surface. Thus the high tides are higher and low tides are lower than normal during a brief period twice each lunar (1) month. Spring tides normally reach their maximum rise 1 to 2½ days after the time of full and new moon. Note that "spring tides" occur several times each month and are not limited to the spring of the year.

Neap Tides

Neap tides occur when the moon and sun are at approximately 90° angles to each other, at which point the tidal effects of the sun and moon oppose each other. This period also occurs twice each lunar month, one or two days following the first and third quarters of the moon. Neap tides are characterized by high tides that are lower than normal and by low tides higher than normal. In other words, there is a smaller "range" (i.e., difference in vertical height) between succeeding high and low tides.

In the following diagram you can see the range of the tide increase as it goes from a neap tide to a spring tide.

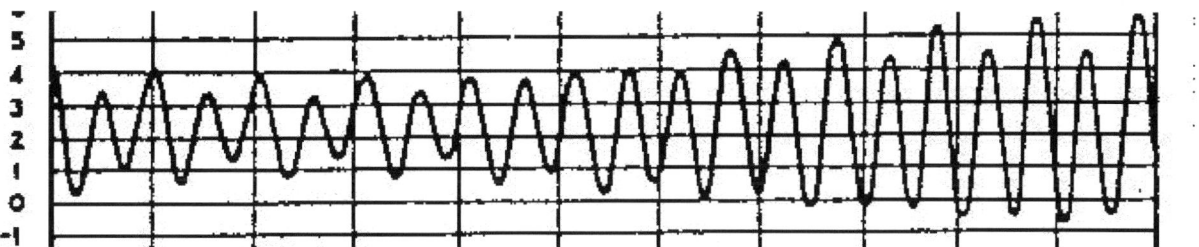

Tidal Datum

Each chart contains a statement that identifies the tidal datum or level from which all heights and depths are measured. In fact, each chart specifies two types of data: the low water datum is the basis from which depths are measured and the high water datum (MHW, MHHW etc.) is the basis from which heights are measured. These data are called "means" or averages. The tides can and do rise above Mean High Water (MHW) and can and do fall below Mean Low Water (MLW). This datum of soundings (i.e., chart datum) is compiled from scientific tidal observations taken over a period of many years. On certain charts, you will see the words "soundings in feet (meters or fathoms) at Mean Low Water." In this case, Mean Low Water (MLW) describes the tidal datum selected as the basis of soundings that appear on that specific chart.

There is a variety of chart datum used throughout the world. Some of the different data in general use are described below. However, the datum used on any given chart is printed on that chart and provides the basis for every sounding on that chart.

- Mean Lower Low Water (MLLW) - the average height of the lower of two low waters at a place. This datum is now used on most charts of U.S.waters.
- Mean Low Water (MLW} - the average height of all low waters at a place. This datum was previously used on many U.S. charts.
- Mean Sea Level (MSL) - the average height of the sea surface for all stages of the tide taken over a 19-year period.
- Mean High Water (MHW) - the average height of all high waters taken over a 19-year period. Elevations are often calculated from this datum.

Tidal Current

Tidal current is the horizontal movement of water that follows and results from the tide's vertical rise and fall. Offshore, the tidal current flows continually with the direction of flow changing through 360 degrees during the tidal period. This is called a rotary current.

Although a tidal current may be related to a type of tide, this relationship is so variable that it is hazardous to try and predict the time and strength of a tidal current from the time of high or low tide. For this reason, you must use the Tide Tables to determine the times and heights of tides and use the Tidal Current Tables to determine the time, set (direction), or drift (speed) of a tidal current.

In rivers, harbors, and straits where the flow is restricted, the tidal current is usually of a reversing nature and is called a reversing current. In other words, the water flows alternately in opposite directions, in and out. Flood is the movement of the tidal current toward the shore or upstream. Ebb is the movement of the tidal current away from shore, out to sea, or downstream. In a reversing current, just before the current changes direction, there is a period of little or no current called slack water. Slack water is also called minimum before flood or ebb.

When dealing with currents there are two quantities needed. Set is the overall direction toward which the water is flowing. Since the terms "flood" and "ebb" are general terms that do not accurately indicate the direction in which the current sets, direction is expressed in degrees true. Drift is the speed the current flows past a given point and is expressed in knots. For our purposes, velocity, speed, and drift are used interchangeably. "Velocity" appears most often in government tidal publications. We prefer to use "speed" to describe "drift" when working DST math problems.

Navigation General Near Coastal
Statements to recognize

Characteristics of Weather Systems

Wind

1. The winds you would expect to encounter in the North Atlantic between latitudes 5° and 30° are known as the **trades.**
2. The horse latitudes are characterized by **weak pressure gradients and light, variable winds**.
3. The doldrums are characterized by **frequent calms**.
4. The wind flow from the horse latitudes to the doldrums is deflected due to **coriolis force**.
5. Weather systems in the middle latitudes generally travel from **west to east**.
6. The pressure gradient between the horse latitudes and doldrums runs **north to south**.
7. Considering the general circulation of the atmosphere, the wind system between latitudes 30°N and 60°N is commonly called the **prevailing westerlies**.
8. A local wind which occurs during the daytime and is caused by the different rates of warming of land and water is a **sea breeze**.
9. **A land breeze** generally occurs when the land is cooler than the nearby water.
10. A sea breeze is a wind **that blows towards an island during the day**.
11. A very light breeze that causes ripples on a small area of still water is a **cat's paw.**

Barometer

12. **The direction and rate of change of barometric pressure** indication on the barometer is most meaningful in forecasting weather.
13. A barometer showing falling pressure indicates the approach of a **low pressure system**.
14. As a high pressure system approaches, the barometer reading **rises**.
15. A slow, gradual fall of the barometer indicates approaching **deteriorating or unsettled weather**.
16. A rapid rise or fall of the barometer indicates **a change in the present weather conditions.**
17. The barometer is an instrument for measuring the **atmospheric pressure.**
18. The purpose of the "set" hand on an aneroid barometer is to **indicate any change in the reading of the barometer.**
19. A rapid change in barometric pressure usually indicates **strong winds.**

Buys Ballot's Law

20. According to Buys Ballot's law, when an observer in the Northern Hemisphere experiences a northwest wind, the center of low pressure is located to the **northeast**.
21. When facing into the wind in the Northern Hemisphere the center of low pressure lies **to your right and behind you**.
22. According to Buys Ballot's law, when an observer in the Northern Hemisphere experiences a northeast wind the center of low pressure is located to the **South-southeast.**

23. If an observer in the Northern Hemisphere faces the surface wind, the center of low pressure is to his **right, slightly behind him**.

Avoiding Storm Center

24. The dangerous semicircle of a hurricane in the Northern Hemisphere is that area of the storm **to the right of the storm's track**.
25. You can determine if your vessel's position is in the dangerous or navigable semicircle of a hurricane by observing whether the wind is veering or backing and plotting two or more recent storm positions from weather bulletins, **both A and B.**
26. In the Northern Hemisphere, the right half of the storm is known as the dangerous semicircle because the wind speed is greater here since the wind is traveling in the same general direction as the storm's track, the direction of the wind and seas might carry a vessel into the path of the storm, the seas are higher because of greater wind speed, **all of the above.**
27. **A veering wind** indicates that you are in a hurricane's dangerous semicircle in the Northern hemisphere.
28. The left half of the storm is called the navigable semicircle because the wind speed is decreased by the storm's forward motion, the wind tends to blow vessels away from the storms track, **both A and B.**
29. In the Northern Hemisphere, if your vessel is in a hurricane's navigable semicircle it should be positioned with the wind on the **starboard quarter, hold course and make as much speed as possible.**
30. In the Northern Hemisphere, if your vessel is in a hurricane dangerous semicircle it should be positioned with the wind on the **starboard bow and heave to until the hurricane has passed.**
31. **A backing wind** suggests that your present position lies in the navigable semicircle of a tropical storm.

Fronts

32. A weather front exists when **air masses of different temperatures meet.**
33. When air masses of different temperatures meet a weather **front** exists.
34. A weather front is **a boundary separating two air masses of different densities.**
35. A boundary separating two air masses of different densities is a **front**.
36. Fronts are represented on a weather map using **symbols**.
37. When two air masses of different densities meet the warmer less dense air is **forced aloft.**
38. When two air masses of different densities meet the colder more dense air is **forced down.**
39. When two air masses of different densities meet the **warmer** less dense air is forced aloft.
40. When two air masses of different densities meet the **colder** more dense air is forced down.
41. Warm moist air is **less dense and lighter than** cold dry air.

42. Cold dry air is **more dense and heavier than** than warm moist air.
43. Regardless of which air mass is advancing the warmer less dense air is always forced **aloft.**

Warm Front

44. When warm air occupies a space formerly occupied by colder air it is a **warm front.**
45. A warm front occurs when **warm air occupies a space formerly occupied by colder air.**
46. On a weather map, a warm front is shown by a **red line with red semicircles pointing in the direction of travel.**
47. The slope of a warm front is about **1 mile vertically to 150 miles horizontally.**
48. The slope of a warm front is **more gradual than** the slope of a cold front.
49. The first indications a mariner will have of the approach of a warm front will be **high clouds gradually followed by lower thicker clouds.**
50. High clouds gradually followed by lower thicker clouds indicate the approach of a **warm front.**
51. As it approaches, a typical warm front will bring **rising temperatures and falling barometric pressure.**
52. Rising temperatures and falling barometric pressure is typical of an **approaching warm front.**
53. Slow moving warm fronts are **less dangerous** than fast moving cold fronts.

Cold Front

54. A cold front occurs when **cold air occupies a space formerly occupied by warm air.**
55. On a weather map, a cold front is shown by a **blue line with blue triangles pointing in the direction of travel.**
56. Fast moving cold fronts are **more dangerous** than slow moving warm fronts.
57. The slope of a cold front is **steeper than** the slope of a warm front.
58. As a cold front passes an observer, pressure **rises and winds become gusty.**
59. After the passage of a cold front the visibility **improves rapidly.**
60. Squall lines with an almost unbroken line of threatening dark clouds and sharp changes in wind direction, generally precede a **fast-moving cold front.**
61. A frontal thunderstorm is caused by **a warm air mass rising over a cold air mass.**

Occluded Front

62. An occluded front occurs when **cold front overtakes a warm front around mature low-pressure areas.**
63. On a weather map, an occluded front is shown by a **a purple line with purple semicircles and purple triangle pointing in the direction of travel.**
64. A purple line with purple semicircles and purple triangle pointing in the direction of travel indicates a **occluded** front on a weather map.

65. With the passage of an occluded front the temperature **drops rapidly.**
66. An occluded front happens when **cold front overtakes a warm front around mature low-pressure areas.**
67. An occluded front usually happens when **cold front overtakes a warm front around mature low-pressure areas.**
68. **An occluded front** forms when a cold front overtakes a warm front around mature low-pressure areas.

Stationary Front

69. A stationary front occurs when **a non-moving (or stalled) boundary between two air masses exists and neither of the air masses is strong enough to replace the other.**
70. When a cold air mass and a warm air mass meet, and there is no horizontal motion of either air mass, it is called a **stationary front.**
71. On a weather map, a stationary front is shown by **an alternating red and blue line with alternating red semicircles and blue triangles on either side of the line.**
72. An alternating red and blue line with alternating red semicircles and blue triangles on either side of the line indicates a **stationary** front on a weather map.

Clouds

Diagram D039NG

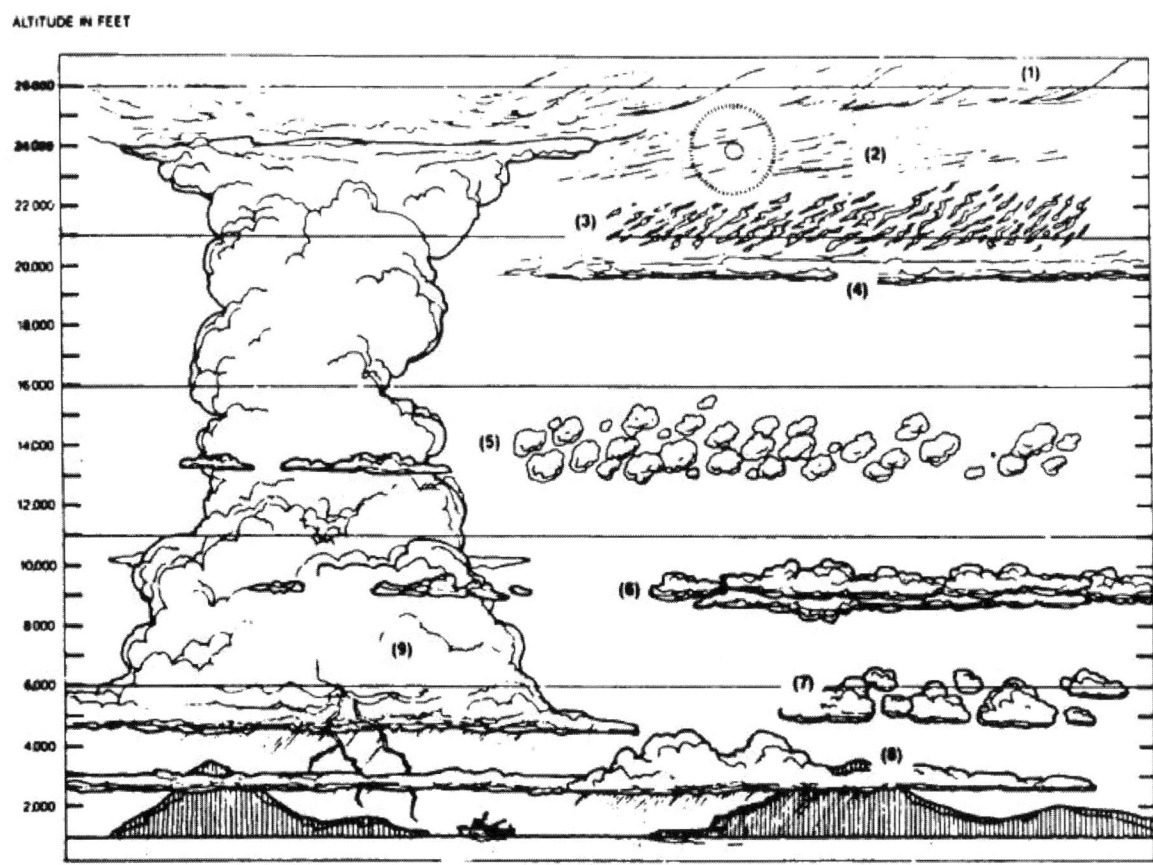

ALTITUDE IN FEET

High Clouds

73. In diagram D039NG, Cirrus Clouds clouds are indicated by number **1**.
74. In diagram D039NG, Cirrostratus Clouds are indicated by number **2**.
75. In diagram D039NG, Cirrocumulus Clouds are indicated by number **3**.
76. Cirrus Clouds are number 1 on diagram D039NG and represent **high clouds**.
77. Cirrostratus Clouds are number 2 on diagram D039NG and represent **high clouds**.
78. Cirrocumulus Clouds are number 3 on diagram D039NG and represent **high clouds**.

Middle Clouds

79. In diagram D039NG, Altostratus Clouds are indicated by number **4**.
80. In diagram D039NG, Altocumulus Clouds are indicated by number **5**.
81. Altostratus Clouds are number 4 on diagram D039NG and represent **middle clouds**.
82. Altocumulus Clouds are number 5 on diagram D039NG and represent **middle clouds**.

Low Clouds

83. In diagram D039NG, Stratocumulus Clouds are indicated by number **6**.
84. In diagram D039NG, Cumulus Clouds are indicated by number **7**.
85. In diagram D039NG, Nimbostratus Clouds are indicated by number **8**.
86. In diagram D039NG, Cumulonimbus Clouds are indicated by number **9**.
87. Stratocumulus Clouds are number 6 on diagram D039NG and represent **low clouds**.
88. Cumulus Clouds are number 7 on diagram D039NG and represent **low clouds**.
89. Nimbostratus Clouds are number 8 on diagram D039NG and represent **low clouds**.
90. Cumulonimbus Clouds are number 9 on diagram D039NG and represent **low clouds**.

Fog

General Fog

91. Fog forms when the air **temperature is equal to, or below the dew point temperature**.
92. When the air temperature is equal to, or below the dew point temperature **fog** forms.
93. Fog forms when the air temperature is at or below **the dew point**.
94. When the air just above the earth's surface is cooled below its dew point by the cooled land **fog forms**.

Radiation Fog

95. Radiation fog forms over low-lying land on **clear calm nights**.
96. As the land radiates heat and becomes cooler, it cools the air immediately above the surface and forms **radiation fog**.
97. The type of fog that occurs on clear nights with very light breezes and forms when the earth cools rapidly by radiation is known as **radiation fog**.
98. Radiation fog **is formed by a temperature inversion**.

Advection Fog

99. **Warm moist air blowing over cold water** is a condition that would most likely result in fog.
100. The fog most commonly encountered at sea is called **advection fog**.
101. The fog produced by warm moist air passing over a cold surface is called **advection fog**.
102. Advection fog may be formed by cold air passing over a **warmer sea surface**.

Compass

Principles of Magnetic Compass

103. The magnetized needle of a compass aligns with **magnetic north and south**.
104. When a compass needle points north is is aligning with **magnetic north and south**.
105. On a magnet like poles **repel** each other.
106. On a magnet opposite poles **attract** each other.
107. Two south poles of a magnet will **repel** each other.
108. Two north poles of a magnet will **repel** each other.
109. The north and south poles of magnets will **attract** each other.
110. The south and north poles of magnets will **attract** each other.

Variation

111. What is variation **the difference between true north and magnetic north**.
112. Variation is determined by the **location of the vessel on the planet**.
113. The location of the ship on the planet determines **variation**.
114. Magnetic compass variation **is the angular difference between geographic and magnetic meridians.**

Deviation

115. What is deviation **is the angular difference between magnetic north and compass north.**
116. Deviation is determined by **the heading of the ship.**
117. The heading of the ship determines **deviation.**
118. Magnetic compass deviation **is the angular difference between magnetic north and compass north.**

Compass Error

119. Compass error is **Variation + deviation = compass error.**
120. Compass error is determined by **adding variation and deviation together.**
121. The compass heading of a vessel differs from the true heading by **compass error.**
122. Compass error is equal to the **combined variation and deviation.**

Charts

Latitude

123. Latitude is on the **vertical axis or sides of the chart.**

124. Vertical axis or sides of the chart indicates **latitude.**
125. Latitude is used to measure **distance** on a chart.
126. Distance is measured on a chart using **latitude**.

Longitude

127. Longitude is on the **horizontal axis or top and bottom of the chart.**
128. Horizontal axis or top and bottom of the chart indicates **longitude.**
129. Longitude specifies **East - West position of a point on a chart.**
130. East - West position of a point on a chart is specified by **longitude**.

Compass Rose

131. The outer ring of a compass rose on a nautical chart provides **true directions.**
132. True directions are provided on a chart by the **outer ring of the compass rose.**
133. The inner ring of a compass rose on a nautical chart provides **magnetic directions.**
134. Magnetic directions are provided on a chart by the **inner ring of the compass rose.**

Aids to Navigation

Starboard Side

135. When returning to a U.S. port the even numbers on the starboard side buoys **increase and the buoys are red.**
136. When returning to a U.S. port the numbers on the red starboard side buoys are **even.**
137. **Lighted red buoys** may be even numbered.
138. The shape associated with starboard side buoys is a **Triangle**.
139. When returning to a U.S. port keep unlighted red **nun** buoys to starboard.
140. Starboard side even numbered aids are **red**.
141. When returning to a U.S. port lighted buoys on the starboard side shall have a **red light.**
142. **Unlingthed nun buoys** may be even numbered.
143. **Lighted red buoys** may be even numbered.
144. Unlighted red buoys have even numbers and are called **nuns**.

Port Side

145. When returning to a U.S. port the odd numbers on the port side buoys **increase and the buoys are green**.
146. When returning to a U.S. port the numbers on the green port side buoys are **odd**.
147. **Lighted green buoys** may be odd numbered.
148. The shape associated with green odd numbered port side buoys is a **square**.
149. When returning to a U.S. port keep unlighted green **can** buoys to port.

150. Port side odd numbered aids are **green**.
151. When returning to a U.S. port lighted buoys on the port side shall have a **green light**.
152. **Unlighted can buoy** may be odd numbered.
153. **Lighted green buoy** may be odd numbered.
154. Unlighted green buoys have odd numbers and are called **cans**.

Preferred Channel

155. Unlighted, red and green, horizontally-banded buoys with the topmost band red **are conical in shape and called nun buoys**.
156. Unlighted, green and red, horizontally-banded buoys with the topmost band green **are cylindrical in shape and called can buoys**.
157. A preferred-channel buoy may be **lettered**.
158. A preferred-channel buoy may show **a red or green light**.
159. A preferred-channel buoy will show a light characteristic of **composite group-flashing (2 + 1) red or green light**.
160. When a buoy indicates the preferred channel is to starboard the topmost band is **green**.
161. When a buoy indicates the preferred channel is to port the topmost band is **red**.
162. A light characteristic of composite group flashing (2 + 1) indicates that there is a **junction in the channel**.
163. Preferred channel buoys indicate the preferred channel to transit by **the color of their top band**.
164. The light characteristic of a lighted preferred-channel buoy is **composite group flashing (2 + 1)**.

Isolated Danger

165. Buoys which mark isolated dangers are painted with alternating **red and black bands**.
166. Buoys which mark isolated dangers have a light characteristic of **Fl (2) Group flashing**.
167. Buoys which mark isolated dangers have a **white** light if lighted.
168. Buoys which mark isolated dangers have a shape on top consisting of **two balls**.
169. Buoys which mark isolated dangers may be **Lettered**.
170. **Fl (2) Group flashing** is the light characteristic of a lighted isolated-danger mark.
171. Isolated-danger marks are **black and red**.
172. The light is **white** on an isolated-danger mark.
173. **Two balls** are on top of isolated-danger marks.
174. Isolated-danger mark may be **Lettered**.

Safe Water

175. A safe water mark may be vertically striped, spherical, showing a white light, **All of the above**.

176. A safe water mark can be passed close aboard on either side and is painted and lighted with **red and white stripes with a white Morse (A) light characteristic.**
177. Safe water buoys may show ONLY **white lights.**
178. A safe water daymark has **octagonal** shape.
179. Under the IALA-A and B Buoyage Systems, a buoy with alternating red and white vertical stripes indicates **that there is navigable water all around.**
180. A lighted safe water mark fitted with **a spherical topmark** to aid in its identification.
181. Buoys which mark safe water may be **lettered.**
182. Lighted buoys which mark safe water have a **white** light.
183. Lighted buoys which mark safe water have **Mo (A) - morse code alfa** characteristic.
184. Buoys which mark safe water are **red and white vertically striped.**

Special Marks

185. Lighted special mark buoys show a **yellow** light.
186. Special mark buoys are **yellow.**
187. Special mark buoys maybe **lettered.**
188. Special mark buoys maybe **nuns or cans.**
189. Special mark buoys must show a light characteristic of **fixed or flashing yellow light.**
190. Under the U.S. Aids to Navigation System, lighted special mark buoys show a **yellow** light.
191. Under the U.S. Aids to Navigation System, special mark buoys are **yellow.**
192. Under the U.S. Aids to Navigation System, special mark buoys maybe **lettered.**
193. Under the U.S. Aids to Navigation System, special mark buoys maybe **nuns or cans.**
194. Under the U.S. Aids to Navigation System, special mark buoys must show a light characteristic of **fixed or flashing yellow light.**

Information and Regulatory Marks

195. White and orange information and regulatory marks may indicate Exclusion area, Restricted operations, Danger, **All of the above.**
196. Exclusion areas, restricted operations and danger may be indicated by a **information and regulatory mark.**
197. Lighted white and orange information and regulatory marks have a **white** light.
198. A white light is displayed by a **lighted white and orange information and regulatory mark.**
199. Lighted information and regulatory mark may display any light characteristic except **quick flashing and flashing (2).**
200. Lighted information and regulatory mark shall not display **quick flashing and flashing (2)** light characteristic.
201. Lighted white and orange information and regulatory mark may display Isophase, Occulting, Flashing, **All of the above** light characteristics.
202. Information and regulatory marks are **white and orange.**
203. White and orange buoys, if lighted, show a **white** light.
204. A white buoy with an orange square on it is an **informational and regulatory buoy.**

Ranges

205.   When you are steering on a pair of range lights and find the upper light is above the lower light you should **continue on the present course.**
206.   You are inbound in a channel marked by a range. The range is in sight and appears vertically aligned. You should **continue on the present heading.**
207.   You are steering on a channel marked by a range. The range is in sight and appears vertically aligned. You should you take **continue on the present heading.**
208.   You are steering on a channel marked by a range. The range is in sight and appears as shown in diagram D047NG. You should **alter course to port and bring the range in line.**

D047NG

209.   You are inbound in a channel marked by a range. The range is in sight and appears as shown in diagram D047NG. You should **alter course to port and bring the range in line.**

D047NG

210.   You are steering on a channel marked by a range. The range is in sight and appears as shown in diagram D048NG. You should **alter course to starboard and bring the range in line.**

D048NG

211. You are inbound in a channel marked by a range. The range is in sight and appears as shown in diagram D048NG. You should **alter course to starboard and bring the range in line.**

D048NG

212. You have steadied up on a range dead ahead in line with your keel. After a few minutes the range, still dead ahead, appears as shown in illustration D047NG. You should **alter heading to the left.**

D047NG

213. You have steadied up on a range dead ahead in line with your keel. After a few minutes the range, still dead ahead, appears as shown in illustration D048NG. You should **alter heading to the right.**

D048NG

214. You have steadied up on a range dead ahead in line with your keel. After a few minutes the range, still dead ahead, appears as vertically aligned with the upper light above the lower light. You should **maintain heading, keeping the range dead ahead.**

Bridges

215. You will know that a swing bridge is open for river traffic at night when **the red light changes to green.**
216. At night you will know that a swing bridge is open for river traffic when **the red light changes to green.**
217. You are approaching a swing bridge at night. You will know that the bridge is open for river traffic when **the red light changes to green.**
218. At night You are approaching a swing bridge. You will know that the bridge is open for river traffic when **the red light changes to green.**
219. You are approaching an open drawbridge and sound the proper signal. You receive no acknowledgment from the bridge. You should **approach with caution and proceed through the open draw.**
220. You sound the proper signal as you are approaching an open drawbridge. You receive no acknowledgment from the bridge. You should **approach with caution and proceed through the open draw.**
221. A drawbridge may use visual signals to acknowledge a vessel's request to open the draw. The signal which indicates that the draw will NOT be opened immediately is a **fixed red light.**
222. To acknowledge a vessel's request to open the draw a drawbridge may use visual signals. The signal which indicates that the draw will NOT be opened immediately is **a fixed red light.**

223. You are approaching a drawbridge and have sounded the proper whistle signal requesting it to open. You hear a signal of one prolonged and one short blast from the bridge. You should **approach under full control to pass through the bridge.**

224. You have sounded the proper whistle signal requesting a drawbridge to open and you are are approaching it. You hear a signal of one prolonged and one short blast from the bridge. You should **approach under full control to pass through the bridge.**

Light Characteristics

225. In the U.S. Aids to Navigation System, lateral aids as seen entering from seaward may display lights with these characteristic; Flashing, Occulting, Quick Flashing, **All of the above.**

226. Lateral aids as seen entering from seaward may display lights with these characteristic in the U.S. Aids to Navigation System; Flashing, Occulting, Quick Flashing, **All of the above.**

227. A light that has a light period shorter than its dark period is described as **flashing.**

228. A lighted buoy that has a light period shorter than its dark period is described as **flashing.**

229. An occulting light is one in which **the period of light exceeds the period of darkness.**

230. An isophase light is one in which **the periods of light and darkness are equal.**

231. A lighted buoy with a fixed light is one in which **the light shows continuously and steady.**

232. The period of a lighted aid to navigation refers to the **time required for the light to complete each cycle.**

233. An alternating light **shows a light that changes color**.

Publications

Light List

234. A Light List is **a detailed list of navigational aids including lighthouses and other lighted navigation aids, unlighted buoys, radiobeacons, daybeacons, and racons.**

235. A Light List is **a detailed list of navigational aids.**

236. **Light List** contains a detailed list of navigational aids.

237. **Light List** contains a detailed list of navigational aids including lighthouses and other lighted navigation aids, unlighted buoys, radiobeacons, daybeacons, and racons.

Coast Pilot

238. **Coast Pilot** contains descriptions of the coast line, buoyage systems, weather conditions, port facilities, and navigation instructions.

239. **Coast Pilot** provides information about channel depths, dangers, obstructions, anchorages, and marine facilities available in that port

240.   **Coast Pilot** contains information on navigation regulations, landmarks, channels, anchorages, tides, currents, and clearances of bridges for Chesapeake Bay.

241.   **Coast Pilot** would describe the explosive anchorages in the ports on the east coast of the United States.

Notice to Mariners

242.   **Notice to Mariners** advises mariners of important matters affecting navigational safety, including new hydrographic information, changes in channels and aids to navigation, and other important data?

243.   Notice to Mariners is used to **learn about important matters affecting navigational safety.**

244.   **Notice to Mariners** advises mariners of important matters affecting navigational safety.

245.   Notice to Mariners is important because it helps boat captains **learn about important matters affecting navigational safety.**

Tides and Tidal Currents

Tide

246.   As the tide rises and falls it is accompanied by a horizontal movement of the water called **tidal current.**

247.   Height of the tide refers to the amount of water in feet above or below the selected **tidal datum.**

248.   The tide rises until it reaches a maximum height called **"high tide" or high water.**

249.   The tide falls until it reaches a minimum height called **"low tide" or low water.**

250.   Tide is the vertical rise and fall of the water caused by **the gravitational "pull" of the moon and sun on different parts of the earth as it rotates through space.**

251.   The gravitational "pull" of the moon and sun on different parts of the earth as it rotates through space causes **tides.**

252.   The range of tide is the **difference between the heights of high and low tide.**

253.   The vertical distance from low water to high water is the **tidal range.**

254.   The term "tide" refer to the **vertical movement of water.**

255.   The height of tide is the **difference between the depth of the water and the area's tidal datum.**

256.   The distance between the surface of the water and the tidal datum is the **height of tide.**

257.   When a current flows in the opposite direction to the waves, the wave **height is increased.**

Semidiurnal

258. Semidiurnal tide has **two high waters and two low waters every tidal day.**
259. A tide with two high waters and two lowaters each tidal day is **semidiurnal.**
260. When a tide has two high waters and two low waters each lunar day it is **semidiurnal.**
261. A semidiurnal tide has **two** high and low waters does a each tidal day.

Diurnal

262. A diurnal tide has **one high water and one low water each tidal day.**
263. A tide is called diurnal when **only one high and one low water occur during a lunar day.**
264. When a tide has only one high water and one low water each lunar day it is **diurnal.**
265. A tide with one high and one low each day is **diurnal.**

Spring Tides

266. Spring tides are tides that **have lows lower than normal and highs higher than normal.**
267. Tides that have higher highs than normal and lower lows than normal are **spring.**
268. Spring tides occur **when the Sun, Moon, and Earth are nearly in line, in any order.**
269. Tides that occur when the Sun, Moon, and Earth are nearly in line are **spring.**
270. Spring tides have a larger **range** than neap tides.

Neap Tides

271. Neap tides are tides that **have lows higher than normal and highs lower than normal.**
272. Tides that have lower highs than normal and higher lows than normal are **neap.**
273. Neap tides occur **when the Sun and Moon are at approximately 90° to each other as seen from the Earth.**
274. Tides that occur when the Sun, Moon, and Earth are at approximately 90° to each other **neap.**
275. Neap tide have a smaller **range** than spring tides.

Current

Set

276. The set of the current is the **direction in which the current flows.**
277. **Set** refers to the direction a current is flowing.

278.   The largest waves (heaviest chop) will usually develop where the wind blows **against the set of the current.**
279.   Tidal current has two components and they are **Set** and Drift.

Drift

280.   Tidal current has two components and they are Set and Drift.
281.   Drift of the current is **its velocity in knots.**
282.   The velocity of the current is its **Drift**.
283.   The current reaches it maximum velocity at **halfway between high and low tide.**

Ebb

284.   Ebb current is **a current going out.**
285.   **Horizontal movement of the water away from the land following high tide** describes ebb current.
286.   A current going out away from land is a **ebb** current.
287.   Horizontal movement of the water away from the land following high tide is an **ebb current**.

Flood

288.   The term "flood current" refers to that time when the water **is flowing towards the land.**
289.   **Horizontal movement of the water toward the land after low tide** describes a flood current.
290.   A current coming in toward land is a **flood** current.
291.   Horizontal movement of the water toward land following low tide is a **flood current.**

Slack

292.   With respect to a reversing current, slack water occurs when there is **little or no horizontal motion of the water.**
293.   When there is little or no movement in a reversing current the current is **slack.**
294.   When it is maximum high tide the current is **slack.**
295.   When it is maximum low tide the current is **slack.**

Tide Tables and Tide Current Tables

296.   Tide Tables are used to **predict tides.**
297.   Tide Table are used to **predict the time and height of a tides at a certain location at any time.**
298.   Tide Current Table are used to **predict tide currents.**
299.   Tide Current Table are used to **predict the set and drift of a current at a certain location at any time.**

Navigation Problems: Chart Plot

Introduction

Navigation Problems Chart Plot is hands on. We spend time plotting navigation questions on a chart. The topics are in a specific order and are designed to build up a skill set while progressing from the easier topics to the harder topics.

You will find that learning to use the charting tools during the first problem set will be the hardest part of the problem set. For example, finding latitude and longitude may prove difficult when you start the first problem set, but by the last problem set you will find it much easier to find latitude and longitude because you are more familiar with the tools and chart.
The following topics are covered in chart navigation:

1. General chart reading
2. True course made good
3. Compass correction
4. Compass course made good
5. Three point fix
6. Distance, speed, and time
7. Estimated time of arrival
8. Speed made good
9. Course to steer with leeway
10. Set and drift

General Chart Reading

The general chart reading section is meant to help students get familiar with the Block Island Sound and Approaches Chart 13205TR that we use in chart plot. All of the questions in this section can be answered using information found on the chart.

General Chart Reading Practice Problems

1. The soundings on this chart are measured in _____.
    a. feet
    b. yards
    c. meters
    d. fathoms

2. You are proceeding from a point 4 miles due east of Montauk Point enroute to Long Island Sound via The Race. You should expect the soundings to _____.
    a. remain fairly constant
    b. increase rapidly at first then remain constant until through the Race
    c. start increasing when north of Montauk Point
    d. be inaccurate due to sound absorption by the mud bottom

3. The precautionary area located in the vicinity of LAT 41°06.1'N, LONG 71°28.8'W informs mariners that _____.
    a. Water depth may vary dramatically in the spring and winter months
    b. Recommended traffic lanes have been established
    c. They are entering into Block Island Sound
    d. Partially submerged hazards to navigation may exist in the area

4. The precautionary area located in the vicinity of LAT 41°06.1'N, LONG 71°28.8'W advises mariners to exercise extreme caution _____.
    a. Avoid this area
    b. Be aware of dangerous wrecks in this area
    c. Exercise extreme care in navigating within this area
    d. Be aware of un exploded mines in this are

5. The broken magenta lines starting at Montauk Point and running generally ENE to Block Island indicate _____.
   a. recommended tracks to Block Island
   b. A submerged cable area
   c. A military exercise area
   d. demarcation lines for application of the COLREGS

6. Areas enclosed by a long and short dashed magenta line indicate _____.
   a. cable areas
   b. dumping grounds
   c. fish trap areas
   d. precautionary areas

7. The chart informs mariners that Plum Island is _____.
   a. dangerous due to strong currents
   b. privately maintained
   c. a wildlife refuge
   d. U.S. Government property and is closed to the public

Answers
   1. A
   2. C
   3. B
   4. C
   5. B
   6. C
   7. D

True Course Made Good

In this type of problem you are usually given a starting point and a finishing point and asked what the True coursed is between the two points. Find the two points and connect them with a straight line. Use your parallel rules to walk to the nearest compass rose to find the true course between the points.

True Course Made Good

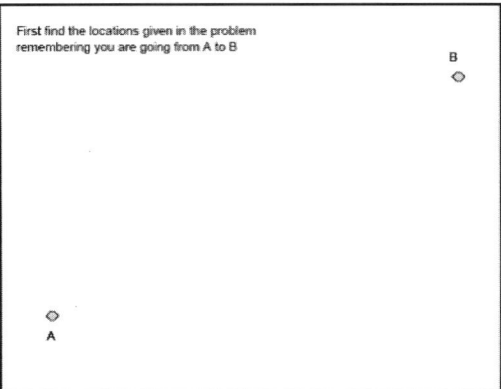

First find the locations given in the problem remembering you are going from A to B

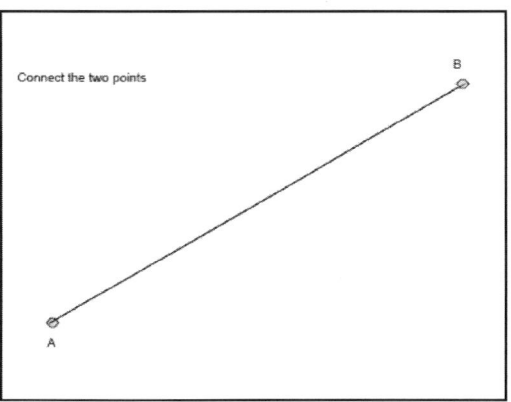

Connect the two points

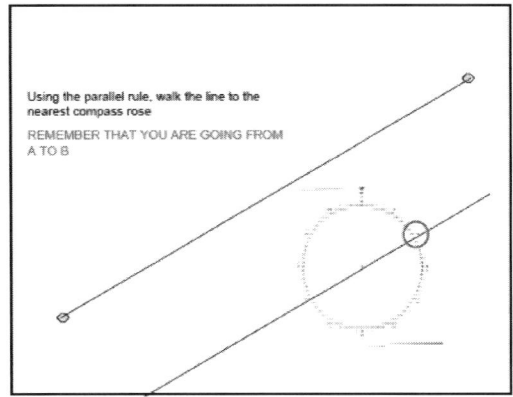

Using the parallel rule, walk the line to the nearest compass rose

REMEMBER THAT YOU ARE GOING FROM A TO B

True Course Made Good Practice Problems

1. At 1016 your GPS position is LAT 41°07.6'N, LONG 71°38.5'W. At 1116 your position is LAT 41°01.4'N, LONG 71°29.4'W. What was the true course made good between the two positions?
    a. 132°T
    b. 135°T
    c. 140°T
    d. 143°T

2. At 1014 you depart the entrance to Lake Montauk with light "1" close aboard. At 1232 your position is LAT 41°20.0'N, LONG 71°40.0'W. What is the true course made good?
    a. 035°T
    b. 039°T
    c. 044°T
    d. 047°T

3. At 0730 your GPS position is LAT 41°16.7'N, LONG 72°06.8'W. At 0800 your position is LAT 41°10.4'N, LONG 71°57.1'W. What was the true course made good between the two positions?
    a. 310°T
    b. 324°T
    c. 131°T
    d. 145°T

4. At 0945 your GPS position is LAT 41°12.1'N, LONG 71°35.6'W. At 1003 your position is LAT 41°15.5'N, LONG 71°34.5'W. What was the true course made good between the two positions?
    a. 014°T
    b. 029°T
    c. 208°T
    d. 194°T

5. At 0005 your GPS position is LAT 41°00.0'N, LONG 71°40.0'W. At 0045 your position is LAT 41°05.1'N, LONG 71°32.9'W. What was the true course made good between the two positions?
    a. 226°T
    b. 241°T
    c. 062°T
    d. 047°T

6. At 2207 your GPS position is LAT 41°05.1'N, LONG 71°32.9'W. At 2405 your position is LAT 41°00.0'N, LONG 71°40.0'W. What was the true course made good between the two positions?
   a. 062°T
   b. 047°T
   c. 226°T
   d. 241°T

7. At 1014 you depart the entrance to Block Island Great Salt Pond with green can buoy "5" close aboard. At 1232 you arrive at the entrance to Quonochontaug Pond. What is the true course made good?
   a. 324°T
   b. 339°T
   c. 158°T
   d. 144°T

Answers
   1. A
   2. B
   3. C
   4. A
   5. D
   6. C
   7. A

Compass Error Correction

Compass error = variation + deviation
CE = V + D

Variation: dependent on **location** and same for all headings
Printed in the compass rose on chart

Deviation: dependent on the **heading** of the vessel
Find deviation on the deviation table

<u>We use a 15°W variation on Block Island Sound and Approaches Chart Problems</u>

Deviation Table

HDG	DEV	HDG	DEV	HDG	DEV
000°	2.0°E	120°	1.0°E	240°	3.0°W
030°	3.0°E	150°	1.0°W	270°	1.5°W
060°	4.0°E	180°	2.0°W	300°	0.0°
090°	2.0°E	210°	3.5°W	330°	1.5°E

Compass correction: TVMDC

			ADD EAST	AT ELECTIONS
TRUE	I	**T** (true)		TWICE
VIRGINS		**V** (variation)		VOTE
MAKE		**M** (magnetic)		MEN
DULL		**D** (deviation)		DEAD
COMPANY		**C** (compass)		CAN
AT WEDDINGS		ADD WEST		

Compass Correction Practice

<u>Use a Variation of 15° W</u>

T _____180°_____   T _____343°_____   T _____42°_____

V _____   V _____   V _____

M _____   M _____   M _____

D _____   D _____   D _____

C _____   C _____   C _____

T _____242°_____   T _____137°_____   T _____8°_____

V _____   V _____   V _____

M _____   M _____   M _____

D _____   D _____   D _____

C _____   C _____   C _____

T _____   T _____   T _____

V _____   V _____   V _____

M _____   M _____   M _____

D _____   D _____   D _____

C _____180°_____   C _____48°_____   C _____350°_____

T _____   T _____   T _____

V _____   V _____   V _____

M _____   M _____   M _____

D _____   D _____   D _____

C _____138°_____   C _____15°_____   C _____283°_____

T _____127°_____   T _____   T _____357°_____

V _____   V _____   V _____

M _____   M _____   M _____

D _____   D _____   D _____

C _____   C _____12°_____   C _____

Compass Correction Practice Solutions

Use a Variation of 15° W

T ___180°___   T ___343°___   T ___42°___

V ___+15°___   V ___+15°___   V ___+15°___

M ___195°___   M ___358___   M ___57°___

D ___+2.8°___   D ___-2°___   D ___-4°___

C ___198°___   C ___356°___   C ___53°___

T ___242°___   T ___137°___   T ___8°___

V ___+15°___   V ___+15°___   V ___+15°___

M ___257°___   M ___152°___   M ___23°___

D ___+2°___   D ___+1°___   D ___-3°___

C ___259°___   C ___153°___   C ___20°___

T ___163°___   T ___36.5°___   T ___337°___

V ___-15°___   V ___-15°___   V ___-15°___

M ___178°___   M ___51.5°___   M ___352°___

D ___-2°___   D ___+3.5°___   D ___+2°___

C ___180°___   C ___48°___   C ___350°___

T ___123°___   T ___2.5°___   T ___267°___

V ___-15°___   V ___-15°___   V ___-15°___

M ___138°___   M ___17.5°___   M ___282°___

D ___0___   D ___+2.5°___   D ___-1°___

C ___138°___   C ___15°___   C ___283°___

T ___127°___   T ___359.5°___   T ___357°___

V ___+15°___   V ___-15°___   V ___+15°___

M ___142°___   M ___14.5°___   M ___12°___

D ___+1°___   D ___+2.5°___   D ___-2.5°___

C ___143°___   C ___12°___   C ___9.5°___

Compass Error Correction Practice Problems

1. Use a variation of 15° W and the deviation table provided in this section. What is your compass heading if your true heading is 180° T?
    a. 162° PSC
    b. 198° PSC
    c. 192° PSC
    d. 168° PSC

2. Use a variation of 15° W and the deviation table provided in this section. What is your compass heading if your true heading is 343° T?
    a. 000° PSC
    b. 330° PSC
    c. 326° PSC
    d. 356° PSC

3. Use a variation of 15° W and the deviation table provided in this section. What is your compass heading if your true heading is 042° T?
    a. 053° PSC
    b. 061° PSC
    c. 031° PSC
    d. 023° PSC

4. Use a variation of 15° W and the deviation table provided in this section. What is your true heading if your compass heading is 048° PSC?
    a. 037° T
    b. 059° T
    c. 067° T
    d. 029° T

5. Use a variation of 15° W and the deviation table provided in this section. What is your true heading if your compass heading is 350° PSC?
    a. 007° T
    b. 003° T
    c. 337° T
    d. 333° T

6. Use a variation of 15° W and the deviation table provided in this section. What is your true heading if your compass heading is 138° PSC?
    a. 223° T
    b. 123° T
    c. 323° T
    d. 153° T

7. Use a variation of 15° W and the deviation table provided in this section. What is your true heading if your compass heading is 015° PSC?
    a. 028° T
    b. 033° T
    c. 003° T
    d. 357° T

Answers
    1. B
    2. D
    3. A
    4. A
    5. C
    6. B
    7. C

Compass Course Made Good

In this type of problem you are usually given a starting point and a finishing point and asked what COMPASS course to steer. Find the two points and connect them with a straight line. Use your parallel rules to walk to the nearest compass rose to find the course between the points. Since you are working on a chart your solution for the course to steer (or heading) from the chart will be in true and you must do a TVMDC to convert to your steering compass.

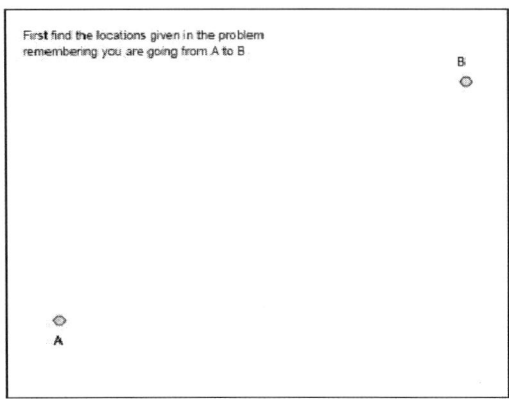

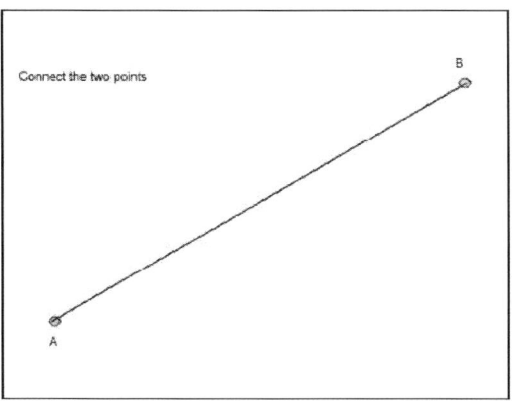

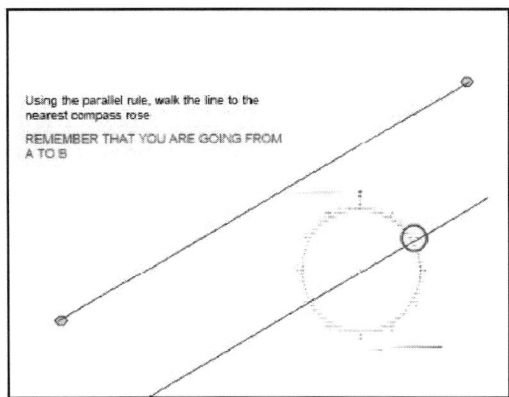

IMPORTANT: This is in **TRUE**

To Correct to **COMPASS** you must do a **TVMDC**

Compass Course Made Good Practice Problems

1. Determine the course per standard magnetic compass from Cerberus Shoal Buoy 9 (LAT 41°10.4'N, LONG 71°57.1'W) to a position 0.2 mile south of Race Rock Light (LAT 41°14.6'N, LONG 72°02.8'W).
   a. 327°psc
   b. 234°psc
   c. 299°psc
   d. 296°psc

2. Determine the course per standard magnetic compass from the entrance to Ninigret Pond (LAT 41°21.3'N, LONG 71°38.3'W) to the entrance to Great Salt Pond on Block Island.
   a. 192°psc
   b. 185°psc
   c. 155°psc
   d. 153°psc

3. You are 3 miles due east of Montauk Point Light. What is the course per standard magnetic compass to a position one mile due south of Block Island Southeast Point Light?
   a. 070°psc
   b. 077°psc
   c. 083°psc
   d. 088°psc

4. You are 3 miles due east of Montauk Point Light. What is the course per standard magnetic compass to LAT 41°00.0'N, LONG 71°40.0'W?
   a. 146°psc
   b. 143°psc
   c. 139°psc
   d. 127°psc

5. You are 3 miles due east of Montauk Point Light. What is the course per standard magnetic compass to a position 0.5 mile due south of Race Rock Light?
   a. 324°psc
   b. 328°psc
   c. 331°psc
   d. 339°psc

6. You are 3 miles due east of Montauk Point Light. What is the course per standard magnetic compass to a position 1.5 miles due east of Watch Hill Point Light?
   a. 017°psc
   b. 013°psc
   c. 101°psc
   d. 006°psc

7. You are 3 miles due east of Montauk Point Light. What is the course per standard magnetic compass to LAT 41°00.0'N, LONG 71°30.0'W?
    a. 108°psc
    b. 122°psc
    c. 124°psc
    d. 130°psc

Answers
    1. A
    2. B
    3. C
    4. B
    5. A
    6. D
    7. B

Three Point Fix

This type of problem allows you to use the bearings of three fixed objects to determine your location on the water. There are a lot of steps to these problems so take your time and be careful. Both bearings and headings are used in these problems. Remember that the only purpose of the heading is to determine the deviation. This deviation will be the same for all bearings. Using TVMDC find the true bearings of the objects given in the problem. Now carefully draw a line from each object using these true bearings. In a perfect world these bearing lines should cross at a point which would be your location. Any slight errors and you will see a triangle formed by the bearing lines. Your position would be assumed to be at the center of this triangle. If this triangle is large, check your work! The answers to these problems are all very close so any careless chart work can yield a wrong answer.

Find the three fixed objects on your chart that are given in the problem.

A   C

B

The psc or COMPASS bearings to these marks are given in the problem.

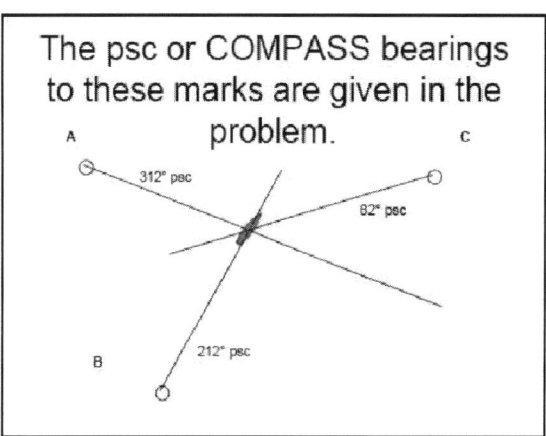

A   C

312° psc   82° psc

212° psc

B

To draw these bearings on a chart, you must convert from psc to **TRUE**.

This is done using TVMDC. Remember that the deviation depends on the boats **HEADING**.

The TRUE bearing does not change with the heading of the boat. Due to the deviation the psc bearing will change with the heading.

The TVMDC will look like this.

We will use a **HEADING of 045°** and we are in a region where the **VARIATION** is **15W**.

	POINT A	POINT B	POINT C
T			
V	15W	15W	15W
M			
D			
C			

The TVMDC will look like this.

Using a **HEADING of 045°** and the deviation table
we find the deviation to be 3E

	POINT A	POINT B	POINT C
T			
V	15W	15W	15W
M			
D	3E	3E	3E
C			

The TVMDC will look like this.

Correct from **COMPASS** to **TRUE**.

These are the lines we can draw on the chart.

		POINT A	POINT B	POINT C
T	↑	300°	200°	070°
V		15W	15W	15W
M		315°	215°	085°
D		3E	3E	3E
C	↑	312°	212°	082°

Once the TRUE Bearings have been determined they are plotted on the chart.

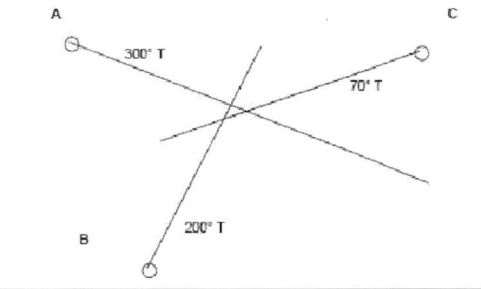

In this case your location is at the center of the triangle formed.

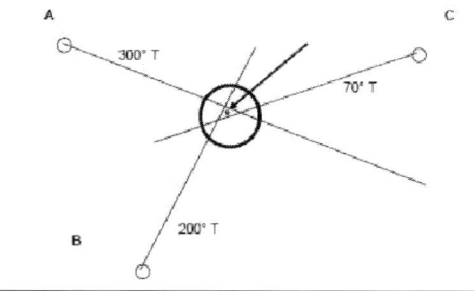

Your Latitude and Longitude are now found by careful use of the parallel rules or dividers and the scales along the edges of the chart.

Three Point Fix Practice Problems

1. You are on course 157° per standard magnetic compass when you take the following bearings: Little Gull Island Light @ 277°psc; Race Rock Light @ 301°psc; Latimer Reef Light @ 028°psc. What is your position?
   a. LAT 41°13.5'N, LONG 71°57.9'W
   b. LAT 41°13.5'N, LONG 71°57.4'W
   c. LAT 41°13.6'N, LONG 71°57.0'W
   d. LAT 41°13.6'N, LONG 71°57.8'W

2. You are on course 137° per standard magnetic compass when you take the following bearings: Watch Hill Point Light @ 051°psc; Montauk Point Light @ 184°psc; Race Rock Light @ 279°psc. What is your position?
   a. LAT 41°15.2'N, LONG 71°54.4'W
   b. LAT 41°15.1'N, LONG 71°53.8'W
   c. LAT 41°15.1'N, LONG 71°54.9'W
   d. LAT 41°15.0'N, LONG 71°53.7'W

3. You are on course 087° per standard magnetic compass when you take the following bearings: Little Gull Island Light @ 277°psc; Race Rock Light @ 303°psc; Latimer Reef Light @ 025°psc. What is your position?
   a. LAT 41°13.1'N, LONG 71°57.5'W
   b. LAT 41°13.1'N, LONG 71°56.9'W
   c. LAT 41°13.0'N, LONG 71°58.0'W
   d. LAT 41°12.9'N, LONG 71°57.2'W

4. You are on course 053° per standard magnetic compass when you take the following bearings: Little Gull Island Light @ 275°psc; Race Rock Light @ 296°psc; Latimer Reef Light @ 011°psc. What is your position?
   a. LAT 41°12.9'N, LONG 71°56.3'W
   b. LAT 41°13.2'N, LONG 71°56.0'W
   c. LAT 41°13.4'N, LONG 71°55.5'W
   d. LAT 41°13.8'N, LONG 71°56.1'W

5. You are on course 246° per standard magnetic compass when you take the following bearings: Little Gull Island Light @ 286°; Race Rock Light @ 308°; Latimer Reef Light @ 018°. What is your position?
   a. LAT 41°12.6'N, LONG 71°55.7'W
   b. LAT 41°12.6'N, LONG 71°56.6'W
   c. LAT 41°12.7'N, LONG 71°56.0'W
   d. LAT 41°13.1'N, LONG 71°56.1'W

6. You are on course 302° per standard magnetic compass when you take the following bearings: Little Gull Island Light @ 283°psc; Race Rock Light @ 311°psc; Latimer Reef Light @ 027°psc. What is your position?
    a. LAT 41°12.2'N, LONG 71°57.6'W
    b. LAT 41°12.4'N, LONG 71°57.4'W
    c. LAT 41°12.4'N, LONG 71°57.9'W
    d. LAT 41°12.7'N, LONG 71°57.7'W

7. You are on course 025° per standard magnetic compass when you take the following bearings: Point Judith Light @ 072°psc; Block Island North Point Light @ 116°psc; Watch Hill Light @ 306°psc. What is your position?
    a. LAT 41°14.9'N, LONG 71°43.2'W
    b. LAT 41°15.1'N, LONG 71°44.0'W
    c. LAT 41°15.4'N, LONG 71°43.1'W
    d. LAT 41°15.6'N, LONG 71°42.8'W

Answers
    1. B
    2. A
    3. A
    4. B
    5. C
    6. D
    7. C

Distance, Speed, and Time

Clock Time vs. Elapsed Time

Clock Times

- in military form (HHMM)
- start times
- arrival time
- estimated arrival time (ETA)

Elapsed Times

- in hours & min
- estimated time en route (ETE)
- time it took to get there
- hours in decimal form are used in Distance, Speed and Time calculations

Time in military form (last two digits are never greater than 59)

Examples:

0001 – 0059   1000 – 1059   2200 – 2259

Remember, in addition and subtraction of times you borrow 60 minutes or carry 1 hour.

$$+\begin{array}{c|c} 11 & 23 \\ 10 & 12 \end{array} \qquad -\begin{array}{c|c} 22 & 55 \\ 20 & 35 \end{array} \qquad +\begin{array}{c|c} 15 & 45 \\ 01 & 25 \end{array} \qquad -\begin{array}{c|c} 09 & 12 \\ 08 & 23 \end{array}$$

Add the following times.

0930 + 2^{hr} 36^{min} 1245 + 4^{hr} 16^{min} 1359 + 36^{min} 1900 + 12^{hr} 30^{min} 2230 + 1^{hr} 36^{min}

Subtract the following times.

1654 − 1245   0130 − 0045   2354 − 1136   1400 − 36^{min} 0138 − 1^{hr} 46^{min}

Solutions

Add	1206	1701	1435	0730 next day	0006 next day
Subtract	$4^{hr}\ 09^{min}$	45^{min}	$12^{hr}\ 18^{min}$	1324	2352 previous

Solutions to Adding and Subtracting Time Section

Adding and Subtracting Time Overview Solutions

$$
\begin{array}{r@{\,}|@{\,}l}
11 & 23 \\
+\ 10 & 12 \\
\hline
\multicolumn{2}{c}{21:35}
\end{array}
\qquad
\begin{array}{r@{\,}|@{\,}l}
22 & 55 \\
-\ 20 & 35 \\
\hline
\multicolumn{2}{c}{02:20}
\end{array}
\qquad
\begin{array}{r@{\,}|@{\,}l}
15 & 45 \\
+\ 01 & 25 \\
\hline
16 & 70 \\
\hline
\multicolumn{2}{c}{17:10}
\end{array}
\qquad
\begin{array}{r@{\,}|@{\,}l}
09 & 72 \\
-\ 08 & 23 \\
\hline
\multicolumn{2}{c}{00:49}
\end{array}
$$

Adding Time Practice Problems Solutions

$0930 + 2^{hr}\ 36^{min}$

$$
\begin{array}{r}
9:30 \\
+\ 2:36 \\
\hline
11:66 \\
\hline
12:06
\end{array}
$$

$1245 + 4^{hr}\ 16^{min}$

$$
\begin{array}{r}
12:45 \\
4:16 \\
\hline
16:61 \\
\hline
17:01
\end{array}
$$

$1359 + 36^{min}$

$$
\begin{array}{r}
13:59 \\
:36 \\
\hline
13:95 \\
\hline
14:35
\end{array}
$$

$1900 + 12^{hr}\ 30^{min}$

$$
\begin{array}{r}
19:00 \\
12:30 \\
\hline
31:30 \\
\hline
7:30 \\
\text{Next Day}
\end{array}
$$

$2230 + 1^{hr}\ 36^{min}$

$$
\begin{array}{r}
22:30 \\
1:36 \\
\hline
23:66 \\
\hline
24:06 \\
\hline
00:06 \\
\text{Next Day}
\end{array}
$$

Subtracting Time Practice Problems Solutions

1654 – 1245	0130 – 0045	2354 – 1136	1400 – 36 min	0138 – 1 hr 46 min
$16:\overset{4}{\cancel{5}}\overset{14}{\cancel{4}}$	$\overset{0}{\cancel{9}}:\overset{8}{\cancel{9}}\cancel{0}$	$23:\overset{4}{\cancel{5}}\overset{14}{\cancel{4}}$	$1\overset{3}{\cancel{4}}:\overset{5}{\cancel{6}}\overset{60}{\cancel{0}}$	$\overset{24}{\cancel{01}}:\overset{9}{\cancel{8}}\overset{8}{\cancel{}}$ $\boxed{23:52}$
$-12:45$	$-:45$	$-11:36$	$-:36$	$-01:46$
$04:09$	$:45$	$12:18$	$13:24$	$23:52$

Converting Hours to Hours and Minutes

You will have to convert hours to hours and minutes to complete Estimated Time of Arrival (ETA) problems. Let us get a bit a practice now.

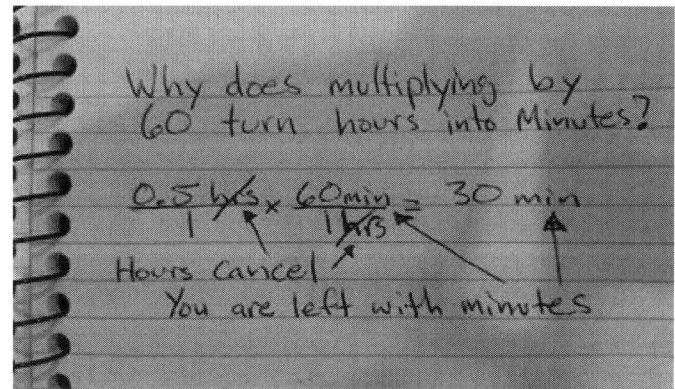

Why does multiplying by 60 turn hours into Minutes?

$0.5 \text{ hrs} \times \frac{60 \text{ min}}{1 \text{ hrs}} = 30 \text{ min}$

Hours cancel
You are left with minutes

Examples

1.5 hrs = _____ hrs _____ min
1 + (.5 hrs * 60) = 1 hr 30 min
1.25 hrs = _____ hrs _____ min

1 + (.25 hrs * 60) = 1 hr 15 min

0.75 hrs = _____ hrs _____ min   2.33 hrs = _____ hrs _____ min   2.65 hrs = _____ hrs _____ min

1.12 hrs = _____ hrs _____ min   3.9 hrs = _____ hrs _____ min   1.1 hrs = _____ hrs _____ min

Answers

0.75 hrs = 0 hrs 45 min	②33 hrs = 2 hrs 20 min	2.65 hrs = 2 hrs 39 min
.75 hr x 60 =	.33 hr x 60 = 20 min	.65 hr x 60 = 39
①12 hrs = 1 hrs 7 min	③.9 hrs = 3 hrs 54 min	①1 hrs = 1 hrs 6 min
.12 hr x 60 = 7.2	.9 hr x 60 = 54	.1 hr x 60 = 6

128

Converting Hours and Minutes to Hours

You will have to convert hours and minutes to hour to complete Speed Made Good (SMG) problems. Let us get a bit a practice now.

Example

$1\ hr\ 20\ min = $ _____ hrs

$20 min \div 60 \frac{min}{hr} = .3\ hrs$

$1\ hr\ 20\ min = 1.3\ hrs$

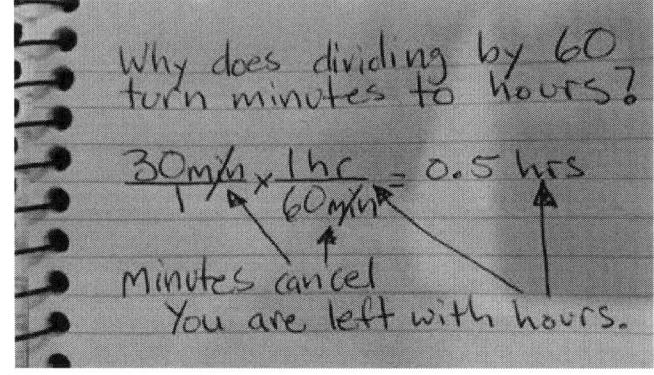

Why does dividing by 60 turn minutes to hours?

$\frac{30\ min}{1} \times \frac{1\ hr}{60\ min} = 0.5\ hrs$

Minutes cancel

You are left with hours.

$1\ hr\ 20\ min = $ _____ hrs $0\ hr\ 45\ min = $ _____ hrs $2\ hr\ 56\ min = $ _____ hrs

$1\ hr\ 8\ min = $ _____ hrs $1\ hr\ 30\ min = $ _____ hrs $3\ hr\ 41\ min = $ _____ hrs

Answers

$1\ hr\ 20\ min = 1.33 hrs$	$0\ hr\ 45\ min = 0.75 hrs$	$2\ hr\ 56\ min = 2.93 hrs$
$\frac{20}{60} = .33$	$\frac{45}{60} \approx .75$	$\frac{56}{60} = .93\ hr$
$1\ hr\ 8\ min = 1.13\ hrs$	$1\ hr\ 30\ min = 1.5\ hrs$	$3\ hr\ 41\ min = 3.68 hrs$
$\frac{8}{60} = .13$	$\frac{30}{60} = .5$	$\frac{41}{60} \approx .68\ hr$

D STREET

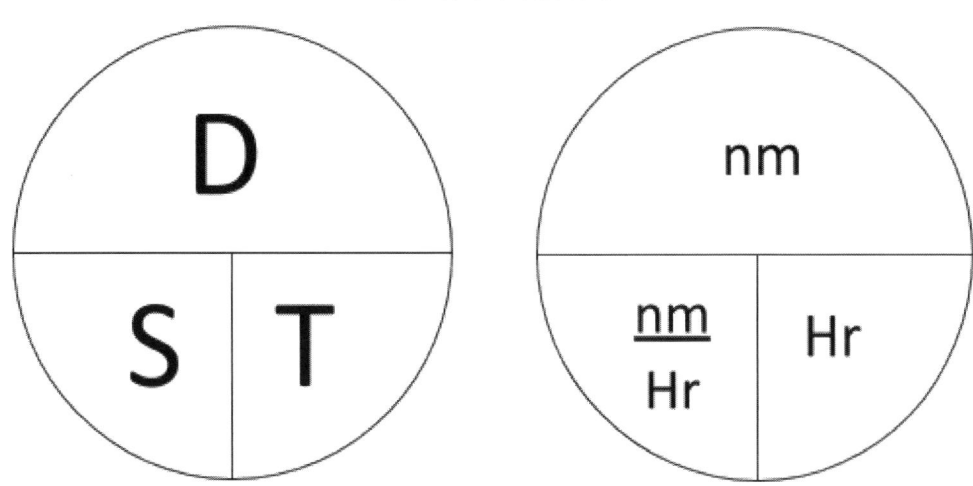

D = distance must be measured in nautical miles

S = speed must be measured in knots (nautical miles per hour)

T = time **must** be measured in hours in **decimal format.**

Time Conversions

HOURS AND MINUTES TO DECIMAL HOURS (DECIMAL ▶ DIVIDE)

OF MINUTES DIVIDED BY 60

45 MINUTES $\qquad \dfrac{45\,MINUTES}{60} = 0.75$ HOURS

3 HR   12 MIN $\qquad \dfrac{12\,MIN}{60} = 0.2$ HR $\qquad$ 3.2 HR

DECIMAL HOURS TO HOURS AND MINUTES (MINUTES ▶MULTIPLY)

DECIMAL PART OF HOURS TIMES 60

0.8 HOURS $\qquad$ 0.8 * 60 = 48 MINUTES

1.3 HOURS $\qquad$ 0.3 * 60 = 18 MINUTES $\qquad$ 1 HR 18 MIN

Estimated Time of Arrival (ETA) Warm up Problems

1. You leave at 6:05, your speed is 18.2 nm/hr and the distance to your destination is 13.3 nm. What is your ETA?

2. You leave at 11:13, your speed is 9.6 nm/hr and the distance to your destination is 17.3 nm. What is your ETA?

3. You leave at 11:03, your speed is 11.3 nm/hr and the distance to your destination is 10.5 nm. What is your ETA?

4. You leave at 10:48, your speed is 8.3 nm/hr and the distance to your destination is 10.4 nm. What is your ETA?

5. You leave at 02:42, your speed is 9.3 nm/hr and the distance to your destination is 8.4 nm. What is your ETA?

Estimated Time of Arrival (ETA) Warm up Problems

1. You leave at 6:05, your speed is 18.2 nm/hr and the distance to your destination is 13.3 nm. What is your ETA?

$$D = 13.3 \text{ nm}$$
$$S = 18.2 \frac{\text{nm}}{\text{hr}}$$
$$T = \frac{D}{S} = .73$$

.73 × 60 = 44 min

```
 6:05
  :44
 ─────
 6:49
```

2. You leave at 11:13, your speed is 9.6 nm/hr and the distance to your destination is 17.3 nm. What is your ETA?

$$D = 17.3 \text{ nm}$$
$$S = 9.6 \frac{\text{nm}}{\text{hr}}$$
$$T = \frac{D}{S} = 1.8 \text{ hr}$$

.8 × 60 = 48 min

```
 11:13
  1:48
 ─────
 12:61
 13:01
```

3. You leave at 11:03, your speed is 11.3 nm/hr and the distance to your destination is 10.5 nm. What is your ETA?

$$D = 10.5 \text{ nm}$$
$$S = 11.3 \frac{\text{nm}}{\text{hr}}$$
$$T = \frac{D}{S} = .93 \text{ hr}$$

.93 × 60 = :56 min

```
 11:03
  :56
 ─────
 11:59
```

4. You leave at 10:48, your speed is 8.3 nm/hr and the distance to your destination is 10.4 nm. What is your ETA?

$$D = 10.4 \text{ nm}$$
$$S = 8.3 \frac{\text{nm}}{\text{hr}}$$
$$T = \frac{D}{S} = 1.25 \text{ hr}$$

.25 × 60 = 15 min

```
 10:48
  1:15
 ─────
 11:63
 12:03
```

5. You leave at 02:42, your speed is 9.3 nm/hr and the distance to your destination is 8.4 nm. What is your ETA?

$$D = 8.4 \text{ nm}$$
$$S = 9.3 \frac{\text{nm}}{\text{hr}}$$
$$T = \frac{D}{S} = .9 \text{ hr}$$

.9 hr × 60 = 54 m

```
 2:42
  :54
 ─────
 2:96
 3:36
```

Estimated Time of Arrival

These problems are very similar to the course per steering compass we just looked at. The difference is once you have located and connected the points you need to measure the distance between the points. You will be given the speed and once you have the distance you can use D-Street to find the ETE. Be sure you know what the problem is asking for. Does it want ETE or ETA? To find the ETA you will add the ETE to the start time.

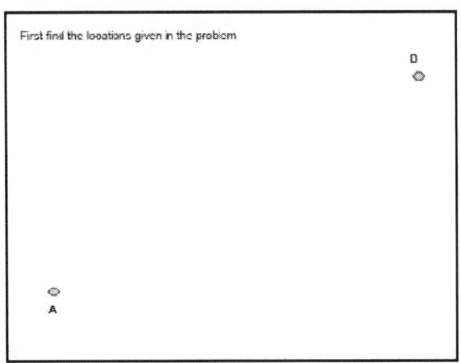

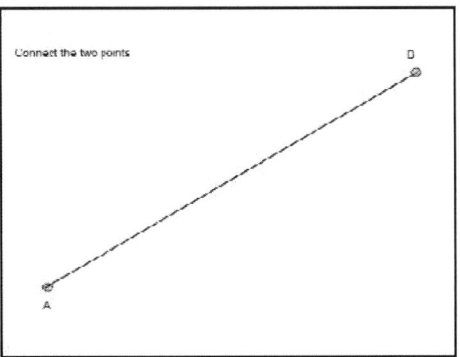

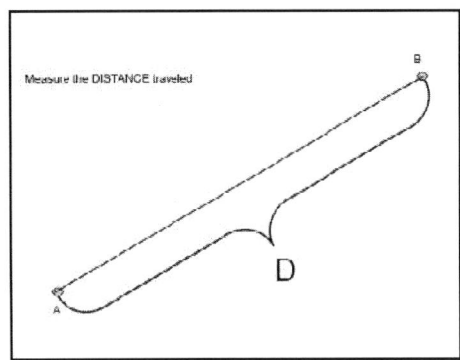

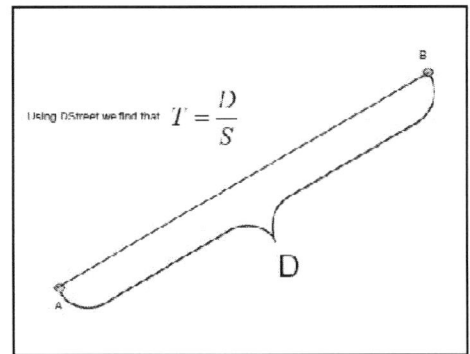

IMPORTANT: This TIME is in **DECIMAL FORMAT**

To find the ETA we must convert this time to

HOURS AND MINUTES

The ETA is found by adding the TIME EN ROUTE just found to the START TIME

Estimated Time of Arrival Practice Problems

1. At 1048 you are in the entrance to Great Salt Pond on Block Island with buoy "5" close aboard. What is your ETA at the west gap of Point Judith Harbor of Refuge if you make good 8.3 knots?
    a. 1149
    b. 1154
    c. 1158
    d. 1203

2. At 1103 your position is LAT 41°12.5 N, LONG 71°37.4 W. What is your ETA at the west gap of Point Judith Harbor of Refuge if you make good 11.3 knots?
    a. 1144
    b. 1154
    c. 1159
    d. 1205

3. At 1103 you are in the entrance to Great Salt Pond on Block Island with buoy "5" close aboard. What is your ETA at light "1" at the mouth of the approaches to Lake Montauk if you make good 8.2 knots?
    a. 1249
    b. 1254
    c. 1259
    d. 1310

4. At 1113 you are in the entrance to Great Salt Pond on Block Island with buoy "5" close aboard. What is your ETA at light "1" at the mouth of the approaches to Lake Montauk if you make good 9.6 knots?
    a. 1310
    b. 1301
    c. 1254
    d. 1249

5. At 2330 your position is LAT 41°16.9' N, LONG 71°38.2' W. You are turning for 9.3 knots. What is your ETA at the entrance to Great Salt Pond on Block Island?
    a. 2355
    b. 0005
    c. 0012
    d. 0019

6. At 1048 you are in the entrance to Great Salt Pond on Block Island with buoy "5" close aboard. What is your ETA at the west gap of Point Judith Harbor of Refuge if you make good 11.3 knots and avoid Block Island North Reef?
    a. 1144
    b. 1154
    c. 1159
    d. 1205

7. Your position is LAT 41°15.2'N, LONG 71°50.1'W at 1347. You are turning for 6.9 knots. What is your ETA at Shagwong Reef Buoy "7SR"?
    a. 1505
    b. 1515
    c. 1521
    d. 1527

Answers

    1. D
    2. C
    3. D
    4. B
    5. B
    6. A
    7. A

Speed Made Good Warm up Problems

1. You depart at 10:14 and arrive at your destination at 12:22 the distance you traveled was 11.7nm. What was your speed made good?

2. You depart at 10:14 and arrive at your destination at 12:38 the distance you traveled was 12.4nm. What was your speed made good?

3. You depart at 10:14 and arrive at your destination at 12:30 the distance you traveled was 19.5nm. What was your speed made good?

4. You depart at 10:16 and arrive at your destination at 11:04 the distance you traveled was 9.9nm. What was your speed made good?

5. You depart at 20:16 and arrive at your destination at 21:28 the distance you traveled was 7.9nm. What was your speed made good?

Speed Made Good Warm up Problems

1. You depart at 10:14 and arrive at your destination at 12:22 the distance you traveled was 11.7nm. What was your speed made good?

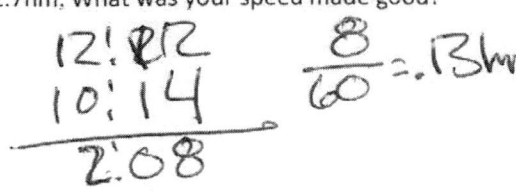

$$12:22$$
$$10:14$$
$$2:08$$

$$\frac{8}{60} = .13hr$$

$$D = 11.7 \frac{nm}{}$$
$$S = \frac{Dnm}{Thr} = 5.5 \frac{nm}{hr}$$
$$T = 2.13hr$$

2. You depart at 10:14 and arrive at your destination at 12:38 the distance you traveled was 12.4nm. What was your speed made good?

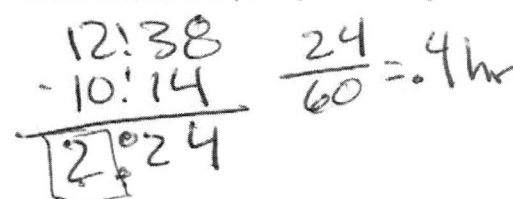

$$12:38$$
$$-10:14$$
$$2:24$$

$$\frac{24}{60} = .4hr$$

$$D = 12.4nm$$
$$S = \frac{D}{T} = 5.2 \frac{nm}{hr}$$
$$T = 2.4 hr$$

3. You depart at 10:14 and arrive at your destination at 12:30 the distance you traveled was 19.5nm. What was your speed made good?

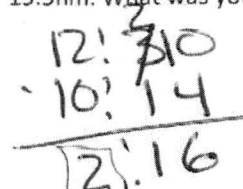

$$12:30$$
$$-10:14$$
$$2:16$$

$$\frac{16mins}{60} = .27hr$$

$$D = 19.5 nm$$
$$S = \frac{D}{T} = 8.6 \frac{nm}{hr}$$
$$T = 2.27 hr$$

4. You depart at 10:16 and arrive at your destination at 11:04 the distance you traveled was 9.9nm. What was your speed made good?

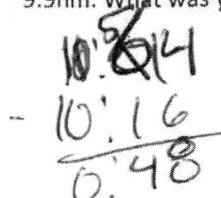

$$10:04$$
$$-10:16$$
$$0:48$$

$$\frac{48}{60} = .8hr$$

$$D = 9.9nm$$
$$S = \frac{D}{T} = 12.4 \frac{nm}{hr}$$
$$T = .8hr$$

5. You depart at 20:16 and arrive at your destination at 21:28 the distance you traveled was 7.9nm. What was your speed made good?

$$21:28$$
$$-20:16$$
$$1:12min$$

$$\frac{12min}{60} = .2hr$$

$$D = 7.9nm$$
$$S = \frac{D}{T} = 6.6 \frac{nm}{hr}$$
$$T = 1.2hr$$

Speed Made Good

These too are very similar to the previous problems. Once the points are connected you can walk the parallel rules to the nearest compass rose and read the true course made good . CAUTION: Look at the answers to see what format they are in, true or psc. Most are true so you are done! For speed made good you need to find the ETE by subtracting the start time from the finish time. Measure the distance traveled. T Then use D-Street to find the speed.

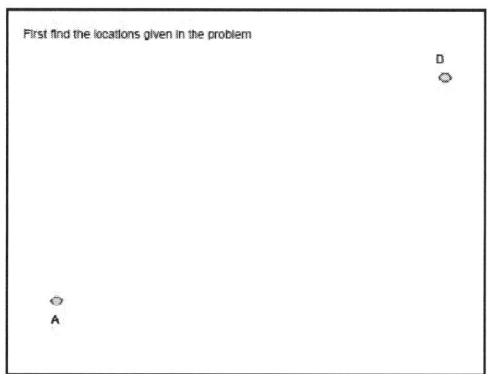

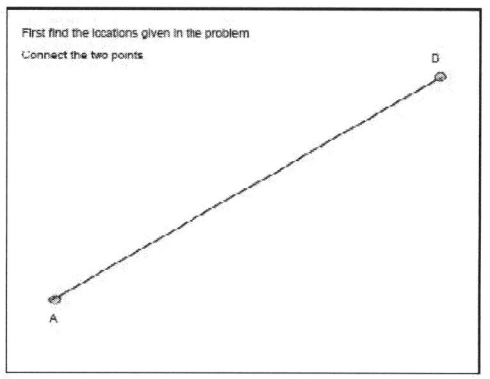

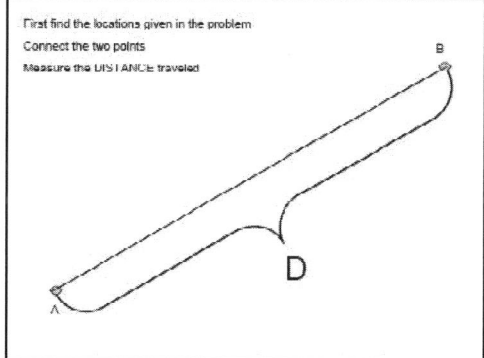

The ETE or ELAPSED TIME is found by subtracting the START TIME from the ARRIVAL TIME

IMPORTANT: This TIME is in **HOURS AND MINUTES**

To use this in a DSTreet calculation, we must convert this time to

DECIMAL FORMAT

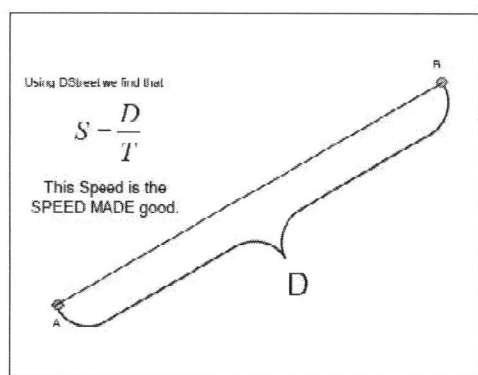

Using DStreet we find that

$$S - \frac{D}{T}$$

This Speed is the SPEED MADE good.

Speed Made Good Practice Problems

1. At 1014 you depart the entrance to Lake Montauk with light "1" close aboard. At 1230 your position is LAT 41°20.0'N, LONG 71°40.0'W. What is the speed made good?
    a. 8.0 knots
    b. 8.3 knots
    c. 8.6 knots
    d. 8.9 knots

2. At 1014 you depart the entrance to Lake Montauk with light "1" close aboard. At 1222 your position is LAT 41°15.8'N, LONG 71°50.9'W. What is the speed made good?
    a. 7.3 knots
    b. 7.5 knots
    c. 5.5 knots
    d. 5.8 knots

3. At 1014 you depart the entrance to Lake Montauk with light "1" close aboard. At 1232 your position is LAT 41°10.4'N, LONG 71°57.1'W. What is the speed made good?
    a. 3.4 knots
    b. 2.4 knots
    c. 3.2 knots
    d. 2.6 knots

4. At 1205 your GPS position is LAT 41°20.0'N, LONG 71°40.0'W. At 1301 your position is LAT 41°10.0'N, LONG 71°50.0'W. What was the speed made good between the two positions?
    a. 12.7 knots
    b. 18.3 knots
    c. 24.3 knots
    d. 13.9 knots

5. At 1014 you depart the entrance to Lake Montauk with Light "1" close aboard. At 1238 your position is LAT 41°20.0'N, LONG 71°40.0'W. What is the speed made good?
    a. 8.9 knots
    b. 8.6 knots
    c. 8.2 knots
    d. 9.2 knots

6. At 1014 you depart the entrance to Lake Montauk with light "1" close aboard. At 1222 your position is LAT41°20.0'N, LONG 71°40.0'W. What is the speed made good?
   a. 8.4 knots
   b. 8.6 knots
   c. 9.2 knots
   d. 9.6 knots

7. At 2016 your GPS position is LAT 41°07.6'N, LONG 71°37.8'W. At 2128 your position is LAT 41°00.4'N, LONG 71°29.4'W. What was the speed made good between the two positions?
   a. 11.9 knots
   b. 10.2 knots
   c. 8.0 knots
   d. 7.4 knots

Answers
   1. C
   2. C
   3. B
   4. D
   5. C
   6. C
   7. C

Course to Steer with Leeway

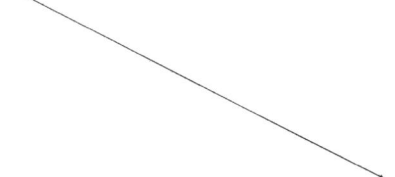

Draw Course Line

1. Draw desired course line

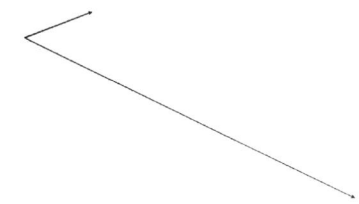

Draw **Current** using **SET** and one hour for the **DRIFT**.

2. Draw Current vector using the SET and one hour if possible to determine length. D = S*T

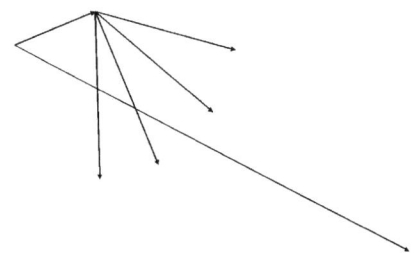

Using Tip of one hour **CURRENT**,

Draw an arc that crosses the course line with a radius equal to the distance the boat can travel in one hour.

3. Determine distance traveled due to boat speed using same time used in "2".
4. Set dividers to this length.
5. Place one point on the tip of the current vector.

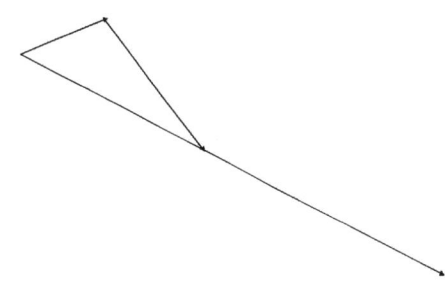

COURSE TO STEER is found by connecting
The tip of the CURRENT to where the
arc crosses the course line.

6. Swing the dividers so that the other point sets on the desired course. Draw a line between these points

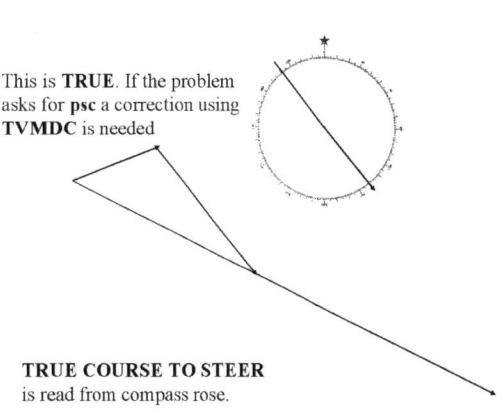

This is **TRUE**. If the problem asks for **psc** a correction using **TVMDC** is needed

7. The Course to Steer is the direction of this line.

TRUE COURSE TO STEER
is read from compass rose.

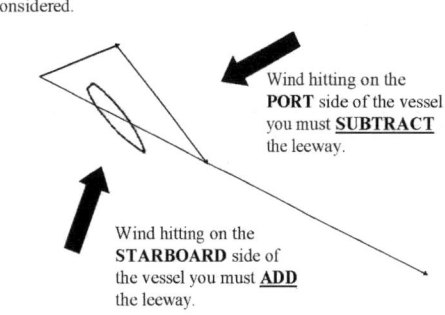

Once this is done then leeway is considered.

Wind hitting on the **PORT** side of the vessel you must **SUBTRACT** the leeway.

8. Leeway: If wind is on port SUBTRACT. If on Starboard ADD

Wind hitting on the **STARBOARD** side of the vessel you must **ADD** the leeway.

142

Course to Steer with Leeway Practice Problems

1. What is the true course to steer between the entrance to Lake Montauk (LAT 41°04.8'N, LONG 71°56.3'W) and Winnapaug Pond entrance (LAT 41°19.6'N, LONG 71°45.8'W), if you are turning for 9.5 knots, allow for a current of 075°T at 1.2 knots, and a westerly wind is causing 3° of leeway?
    a. 020°T
    b. 023°T
    c. 026°T
    d. 029°T

2. What is the true course to steer between the entrance to Winnapaug Pond (LAT 41°19.6'N, LONG 71°45.8'W) and the entrance to Lake Montauk (LAT 41°04.8'N, LONG 71°56.3'W), if you are turning for 6.5 knots, allow for a current of 295°T at 0.9 knot, and an easterly wind is causing 4° of leeway?
    a. 196°T
    b. 200°T
    c. 213°T
    d. 217°T

3. Your position is 3 miles due east of Montauk Point Light. What is the course to steer to arrive at LAT 41°00.0'N, LONG 71°30.0'W, if you are turning for 8.7 knots, the current is 130°T at 1.2 knots, and a northerly wind causes 3° of leeway?
    a. 112°T
    b. 108°T
    c. 105°T
    d. 102°T

4. Your position is 3 miles due east of Montauk Point Light. What is the course to steer to arrive at LAT 41°00.0'N, LONG 71°30.0'W, if you are turning for 7.8 knots, the current is 130°T at 1.2 knots, and a southerly wind causes 3° of leeway?
    a. 112°T
    b. 108°T
    c. 105°T
    d. 102°T

5. Your position is 3 miles due east of Montauk Point Light. What is the true course to steer to arrive at LAT 41°00.0'N, LONG 71°30.0'W, if you are turning for 7.8 knots, the current is 330°T at 1.2 knots, and a southerly wind causes 3° of leeway?
    a. 117°T
    b. 112°T
    c. 104°T
    d. 102°T

6. What is the true course to steer between the entrance to Great Salt Pond (LAT 41°12.0'N, LONG 71°35.6'W) and the entrance to Quonochontaug Pond (LAT 41°19.8'N, LONG 71°43.2'W), if you are turning for 8.5 knots, and you allow for a current of 247°T at 1.2 knots, and an easterly wind is causing 2° of leeway?
    a. 314°T
    b. 320°T
    c. 328°T
    d. 333°T

7. You are turning for 7.5 knots and a westerly wind is causing 2° of leeway. There is a current of 047°T at 1.2 knots. What course should you steer between the entrance to Quonochontaug Pond (LAT 41°19.8'N, LONG 71°43.2'W) and the entrance to Great Salt Pond (LAT 41°12.0'N,;LONG 71°35.6'W).
    a. 162°T
    b. 154°T
    c. 144°T
    d. 140°T

Answers
    1. A
    2. A
    3. D
    4. B
    5. A
    6. D
    7. B

Set and Drift

A   DR

1. Draw DR line

Find Start point "A" and draw DR line.
This is a **TRUE** compass course
or a course **TO** a given point.

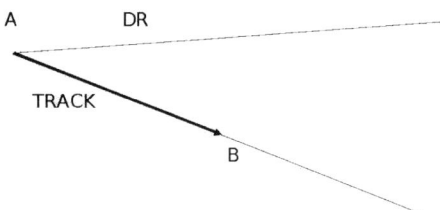

2. Plot the actual "FIX" and draw a track
   (TR) line

The Boat has FOLLOWED the track from "A" to "B"

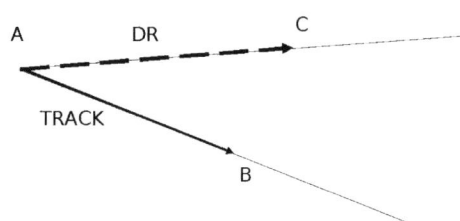

3. Determine distance traveled due to boat
   speed. USE ELAPSED TIME HERE.
Plot this DR position **ON** the DR line.

Calculate DR position "C" using **same time** as "B". Plot **ON** DR line.
(this is where you thought you should be)

145

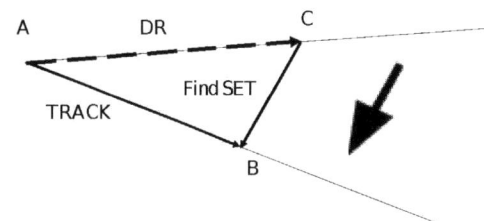

4. SET is determined by connecting this DR position (C) to the FIX position (B) and reading direction from a compass rose

Connect "C" to "B". SET is direction **from** "C" to "B".
To find direction use parallel rules and walk to compass rose.

5. Now determine the DRIFT.

Determine a one hour DR position and plot it **ON** the DR line.

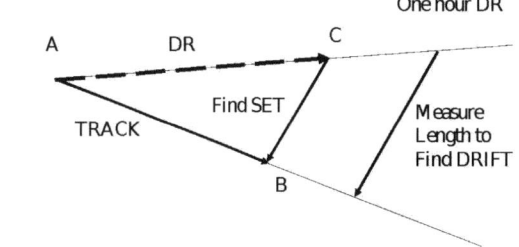

Line up your parallel rule with the SET and walk this direction to the one hour DR point.

Using One hour determine DR position and plot **ON** DR line.
Draw a line from this point parallel to SET.

K Stepnitz 4-15-2005

Draw a line from the DR point that crosses the track line.

The distance between the DR point and the track line ALONG this line represents the DRIFT.

Set and Drift Practice Problems

1. At 1516 your position is LAT 41°11.3'N, LONG 71°48.6'W. You are on course 300° per standard magnetic compass at 9.4 knots. At 1600 your position is LAT 41°14.0'N, LONG 71°58.1'W. What were the set and drift?
    a. 142°T at 1.9 knots
    b. 153°T at 1.4 knots
    c. 332°T at 1.5 knots
    d. 347°T at 1.1 knots

2. At 2038 your position is LAT 41°09.2'N, LONG 71°40.6'W. You are on course 301° per standard magnetic compass at 7.2 knots. At 2152 your position is LAT 41°11.3'N, LONG 71°48.6'W. What were the set and drift?
    a. 080°T at 1.0 knot
    b. 096°T at 2.0 knots
    c. 261°T at 1.2 knots
    d. 277°T at 0.9 knots

3. At 0726 you depart Lake Montauk with light 1 close aboard and set course 065° per standard magnetic compass at 6.7 knots. At 0912 your GPS position is LAT 41°12.8'N, LONG 71°48.2'W. What are the set and drift of the current?
    a. 151°T at 1.0 knots
    b. 287°T at 2.0 knots
    c. 164°T at .07 knots
    d. 321°T at 0.8 knots

4. At 1922 your position is LAT 41°09.2'N, LONG 71°40.6'W. You are on course 028° per standard magnetic compass at 6.4 knots. At 2046 your position is LAT 41°17.2'N, LONG 71°38.6'W. What were the set and drift?
    a. 235°T at 0.8 knots
    b. 247°T at 1.1 knots
    c. 049°T at 0.7 knots
    d. 062°T at 1.0 knots

5. At 0726 you depart Lake Montauk with light 1 close aboard and set course 309° per standard magnetic compass at 6.7 knots. At 0818 your GPS position is LAT 41°07.1'N, LONG 72°02.6'W. What is the current?
    a. 106°T at 0.6 knots
    b. 164°T at 0.7 knots
    c. 334°T at 0.9 knots
    d. 321°T at 0.6 knots

6. At 0726 you depart Lake Montauk with light 1 close aboard and set course 065° per standard magnetic compass at 6.7 knots. At 0912 your GPS position is LAT 41°10.5'N, LONG 71°46.6'W. What is the current?
    a. 151°T at 1.2 knots
    b. 164°T at 0.7 knots
    c. 227°T at 0.9 knot s
    d. 240°T at 1.4 knots

7. At 0726 you depart Lake Montauk with light 1 close aboard and set course 310.5° per standard magnetic compass at 7.6 knots. At 0812 your GPS position is LAT 41°08.1'N, LONG 72°03.7'W. What is the current?
    a. 330°T at 1.1 knots
    b. 164°T at 0.7 knots
    c. 151°T at 1.0 knot
    d. 321°T at 0.8 knots

Answers
    1. C
    2. B
    3. B
    4. A
    5. A
    6. D
    7. A

Navigation Problems Chart Plot Statements to Recognize

General Chart Reading

1. According to NOTE B, THE U.S. NAVAL AIRCRAFT GARDINER'S POINT TARGET is a dangerous due to **live undetonated explosives**.
2. Soundings indicated by a blue tint on this chart are **30 feet or less.**
3. The soundings on this chart are measured in **feet.**
4. Sounding contour lines are at **30 foot intervals** in water with no blue tint.

True Course Made Good

5. At 1016 your GPS position is LAT 41°07.6'N, LONG 71°37.9'W. At 1104 your position is LAT 41°00.2'N, LONG 71°29.4'W. The true course made good between the two positions was **139°T.**
6. At 2302 your GPS position is LAT 41°15.5'N, LONG 71°34.5'W. At 0004 your position is LAT 41°12.1'N, LONG 71°35.6'W. The true course made good between the two positions was **194°T.**
7. At 1014 you depart the entrance to Quonochontaug Pond. At 1232 you arrive at the entrance to Block Island Great Salt Pond with green can buoy "5" close aboard. The true course made good was **144°T.**
8. At 1016 your GPS position is LAT 41°07.6'N, LONG 71°38.5'W. At 1116 your position is LAT 41°01.4'N, LONG 71°29.4'W. The true course made good between the two positions was **132°T.**

Compass Correction

9. Use a variation of 15° W and the deviation table provided in this section. If your true heading is 242° T your compass heading is **259° PSC.**
10. Use a variation of 15° W and the deviation table provided in this section. If your true heading is 137° T your compass heading is **153° PSC.**
11. Use a variation of 15° W and the deviation table provided in this section. If your compass heading is 180° PSC your compass heading is **163° T.**
12. Use a variation of 15° W and the deviation table provided in this section. If your true heading is 180° T your compass heading is **198° PSC.**

Compass Course Made Good

13. The course per standard magnetic compass from 0.2 mile south of Race Rock Light (LAT 41°14.6'N, LONG 72°02.8'W) to the entrance of the channel to Lake Montauk (west of Montauk Point) is **169°psc.**

14. The course per standard magnetic compass from Cerberus Shoal Buoy "9" (LAT 41°10.4'N, LONG 71°57.1'W) to the entrance to Quonochontaug Pond (LAT 41°19.8'N, LONG 71°43.2'W) is **059°psc.**

15. The course per standard magnetic compass from the entrance to Quonochontaug Pond (LAT 41°19.8'N, LONG 71°43.2'W) to the entrance to Great Salt Pond on Block Island is **161°psc**.

16. The course per standard magnetic compass from Cerberus Shoal Buoy 9 (LAT 41°10.4'N, LONG 71°57.1'W) to a position 0.2 mile south of Race Rock Light (LAT 41°14.6'N, LONG 72°02.8'W) is **327°psc.**

Three Point Fix

17. You are on course 298° per standard magnetic compass when you take the following bearings: Block Island Southeast Point Light @ 058° psc; Block Island Aero Beacon @ 005° psc; Montauk Point Light @ 268° psc. Your position is **LAT 41°08.2'N, LONG 71°34.4'W.**

18. You are on course 282° per standard magnetic compass when you take the following bearing: Point Judith Light @ 073° psc; Block Island North Light @ 156° psc; Watch Hill Point Light @ 293° psc. Your position is **LAT 41°17.0'N, LONG 71°38.2'W.**

19. You are on course 073° per standard magnetic compass when you take the following bearings: Watch Hill Point Light @ 037°psc; Montauk Point Light @ 179°psc; Race Rock Light @ 289°psc. Your position is **LAT 41°13.8'N, LONG 71°54.3'W.**

20. You are on course 157° per standard magnetic compass when you take the following bearings: Little Gull Island Light @ 277°psc; Race Rock Light @ 301°psc; Latimer Reef Light @ 028°psc. Your position is **LAT 41°13.5'N, LONG 71°57.4'W.**

Distance, Speed, and Time

21. You leave at 6:15, your speed is 11.8 nm/hr and the distance to your destination is 25 nm. Your ETA is **8:22.**

22. You depart at 11:14 and arrive at your destination at 12:22 the distance you traveled was 11.7nm. Your speed made good is **10.4 knots.**

23. You leave at 23:00, your speed is 6.2 nm/hr and the distance to your destination is 86 nm. Your ETA is **12:52.**

24. You leave at 11:03, your speed is 11.3 nm/hr and the distance to your destination is 10.5 nm. Your ETA is **11:59.**

Estimated Time of Arrival

25. At 1523 your position is LAT 41°08.2'N, LONG 71°34.4'W. You are turning for 8.7 knots. Your ETA at Shagwong Reef Buoy "7SR" is **1711.**
26. At 0242 your position is LAT 41°16.8'N, LONG 71°39.9'W. You are turning for 9.3 knots. Your ETA at the West Gap of Pt. Judith Harbor of Refuge is **03:36.**
27. At 06:05 you are at the mouth of the approaches to Lake Montauk with light "1" close aboard. Your ETA at Watch Hill Reef buoy "1" if you make good 18.2 knots is **06:49.**
28. At 1048 you are in the entrance to Great Salt Pond on Block Island with buoy "5" close aboard. Your ETA at the west gap of Point Judith Harbor of Refuge if you make good 8.3 knots is **1203.**

Speed Made Good

29. At 2016 your GPS position is LAT 41°07.6'N, LONG 71°33.8'W. At 2128 your position is LAT 41°00.4'N, LONG 71°29.4'W. The speed made good between the two positions is **6.7 knots.**
30. At 1016 your GPS position is LAT 41°07.6'N, LONG 71°38.5'W. At 1104 your position is LAT 41°00.4'N, LONG 71°29.4'W. The speed made good between the two positions is **12.5 knots.**
31. At 1014 you depart the entrance to Lake Montauk with Light "1" close aboard. At 1238 your position is LAT 41°16.1'N, LONG 71°49.2'W. The speed made good between the two positions is **5.2 knots.**
32. At 1014 you depart the entrance to Lake Montauk with light "1" close aboard. At 1230 your position is LAT 41°20.0'N, LONG 71°40.0'W. The speed made good between the two positions is **8.6 knots.**

Course to Steer with Leeway

33. The true course to steer between the entrance to Winnapaug Pond (LAT 41°19.6'N, LONG 71°45.8'W) and the entrance to Lake Montauk (LAT 41°04.8'N, LONG 71°56.3'W), if you are turning for 8.5 knots, allowing for a current of 095°T at 0.9 knot, and an easterly wind is causing 3° of leeway is **211°T.**
34. Your position is 3 miles due east of Montauk Point Light. The course to steer to arrive one mile due south of Block Island Southeast Point Light, if you are turning for 8.6 knots, the current is 130°T at 1.2 knots, and a northerly wind causes 3° of leeway is **061°T.**
35. Your position is 3 miles due east of Montauk Point Light. The true course to steer to arrive one mile due south of Block Island Southeast Point Light, if you are turning for 6.8 knots, the current is 330° T at 1.2 knots, and a southerly wind causes 3° of leeway is **084°T.**

36. The true course to steer between the entrance to Lake Montauk (LAT 41°04.8'N, LONG 71°56.3'W) and Winnapaug Pond entrance (LAT 41°19.6'N, LONG 71°45.8'W), if you are turning for 9.5 knots, allow for a current of 075°T at 1.2 knots, and a westerly wind is causing 3° of leeway is **020°T.**

Set and Drift

37. At 0947 your position is LAT 41°15.9'N, LONG 71°41.7'W. You are on course 182° per magnetic compass at 11.3 knots. At 1020 your position is LAT 41°09.2'N, LONG 71°40.6'W. The set and drift are **229°T at 2.0 knots.**

38. At 07:27 you depart Lake Montauk with light 1 close aboard and set course 013.5° per standard magnetic compass at 7.6 knots. At 0812 your GPS position is LAT 41°09.7'N, LONG 71°55.2'W. The set and drift are **141°T at 1.3 knots.**

39. At 1020 your position is LAT 41°11.0'N, LONG 71°50.0'W. You are on course 056° per standard magnetic compass at 9.2 knots. At 1112 your position is LAT 41°15.9'N, LONG 71°41.7'W. The set and drift are **141°T at 1.2 knots.**

40. At 1516 your position is LAT 41°11.3'N, LONG 71°48.6'W. You are on course 300° per standard magnetic compass at 9.4 knots. At 1600 your position is LAT 41°14.0'N, LONG 71°58.1'W. The set and drift are **332°T at 1.5 knots.**

Deck General / Safety

Seamanship

Marlinspike Seamanship

Back in the day of sailing ships there were many lines that needed to be worked with aboard a vessel. A sailor's skill level was often judged on his ability to work with these lines. This ability is called marlinespike seamanship, and it can also be defined as the set of processes and skills used to make, repair, and use rope. This includes tying knots, splicing, and proper use and storage of rope.

Ropes and Lines

A rope is a length of fibers, twisted or braided together to improve strength for pulling and connecting. It has tensile strength but it is too flexible to provide compression strength. The materials used to make rope are either natural or synthetic fibers. The natural fibers include manila, hemp, cotton, coir, jute, sisal, and flax. These natural fibers are being phased out by synthetic fiber. The synthetic fibers used to make rope are polypropylene, nylon, Dacron, polyesters (Vectran), polyethylene (Spectra and Dyneema), and aramid (Kevlar). Some rope is made of a combination of several fibers or the use of co-polymer fibers.

"Rope" refers to the manufactured material. Once a rope is cut to size and assigned a purpose it is referred to as a "line". Some typical lines found on a fishing vessel are fishing line, dock line, anchor line, and downrigger line. Sailing vessels have many lines on board and they are assigned names based on what purpose they serve. For example, halyards raise sails, sheets control the trim of a sail, a downhaul pulls a sail down, and furling lines furl sails.

Minimum Breaking Strength (MBS)

Lines are regularly put under stress when they are in use. The stress at which a line fractures is called the minimum breaking strength (MBS). The MBS of a line depends on the type of fiber from which the line made and the diameter of the line. Other appliances used on boats have a MBS such as hooks, shackles, cable, and chain. The MBS of shackles are higher than hooks of the same diameter, and the MBS of synthetic lines are higher than those of natural fiber line of the same diameter. Sunlight is most likely to impair the strength and durability of synthetic line, while rot is most likely to impair the strength of natural fiber line.

Chafing Gear

When a vessel is moored in the same position for long periods of time or repeatedly in the same position, the mooring lines that hold the vessel in place wear in the same areas and will eventually part the line. To prevent the lines from chafing and parting, chafing gear is wrapped around the line at the wear points. Chafing gear is a covering (usually rope or canvas) of a line or spar to protect it from friction. Chafing gear should be placed at all wearing points of mooring lines and is normally used on mooring lines. It also reduces and prevents wear caused by the rubbing of one object against another. Old fire hose makes excellent chafing gear.

Terms and Definitions

- One or more sheaves fitted in a wood or metal frame is a Block.
- A smooth, tapered pin, usually of wood, used to open up the strands of a rope for splicing is called a(n) fid.
- A deck fitting, used to secure line or wire rope, consisting of a single body with two protruding horns is called a cleat.
- This statement is TRUE about hooks and shackles, Shackles are stronger than hooks of the same diameter.

Watchkeeping

Basics of Watchkeeping

Watchstanding, or watchkeeping, in nautical terms concerns the division of qualified personnel to operate a ship continuously.

In this Schedule in its application to a ship without a bridge, the word "bridge" shall be construed as meaning the position from which the navigation of the ship is controlled.

Part 1 - Voyage Planning

1. General requirements

(1) The intended voyage shall be planned in advance, taking into consideration all pertinent information, and any course laid down shall be checked before the voyage commences.

(2) The chief engineer officer shall, in consultation with the master, determine in advance the needs of the intended voyage, taking into consideration the requirements for fuel, water, lubricants, chemicals, expendable and other spare parts, tools, supplies and any other requirements.

2. Planning prior to each voyage

Prior to each voyage the master of every ship shall ensure that the intended route from the port of departure to the first port of call is planned using adequate and appropriate charts and other nautical publications necessary for the intended voyage, containing accurate, complete and up-to-date information regarding those navigational limitations and hazards which are of a permanent or predictable nature and which are relevant to the safe navigation of the ship.

3. Verification and display of planned route

When the route planning is verified taking into consideration all pertinent information, the planned route shall be clearly displayed on appropriate charts and shall be continuously available to the officer in charge of the watch, who shall verify each course to be followed prior to using it during the voyage.

4. Deviation from planned route

If a decision is made, during a voyage, to change the next port of call of the planned route, or if it is necessary for the ship to deviate substantially from the planned route for other reasons, then an amended route shall be planned prior to deviating substantially from the route originally planned.

Part 2 - Watchkeeping at Sea

1. Principles applying to watchkeeping generally

The master of every ship shall ensure that watchkeeping arrangements are adequate for maintaining a safe navigational watch. Under the master's general direction, the officers of the navigational watch are responsible for navigating the ship safely during their periods of duty, when they will be particularly concerned with avoiding collision and stranding.

2. Protection of marine environment

The master, officers and ratings shall be aware of the serious effects of operational or accidental pollution of the marine environment and shall take all possible precautions to prevent such pollution, particularly within the framework of relevant international and port regulations.

Part 3 - Principles to Be Observed In Keeping a Navigational Watch

1. General

The officer in charge of the navigational watch is the master's representative and is primarily responsible at all times for the safe navigation of the ship and for complying with the requirements in force of the International Regulations for Preventing Collisions at Sea 1972 .

2. Look-out

(1) A proper look-out shall be maintained at all times in compliance with rule 5 of the International Regulations for Preventing Collisions at Sea 1972 and shall serve the purpose of-

(a) maintaining a continuous state of vigilance by sight and hearing as well as by all other available means, with regard to any significant change in the operating environment;

(b) fully appraising the situation and the risk of collision, stranding and other dangers to navigation; and

(c) detecting ships or aircraft in distress, shipwrecked persons, wrecks, debris and other hazards to safe navigation.

Helpful Tip

Be sure to review the Statements to Recognize for Watchkeeping.

Vessel Maneuvering and Handling

Vessel Handling in Rivers and Estuaries

Rivers and Estuaries

Some of our major ports are located on rivers or estuaries. An estuary is a partially enclosed coastal body of brackish water with one or more rivers or streams flowing into it, and with a free connection to the open sea. A river is a natural flowing watercourse, usually freshwater, flowing towards an ocean, sea, lake or another river. When handling a ship in rivers and estuaries captains should be aware of dynamic currents and ever changing water levels which affect the clearance heights of bridges.

Current

Current is a significant factor when maneuvering in a river or estuary. Ship handlers must determine the set and drift of the current and consider it in every maneuver. A good way to get a sense for the speed and direction of the current is to watch the current's wake at a buoy or piling. A rule of thumb is that a 1-knot current causes a definite ripple in the water, a 3-knot current will cause swirls and eddies for several yards and a 5-knot current will cause a V-shaped boiling wake for almost 50 yards downstream with the point of the "V" pointing upstream.

Winding river currents tend to cause the greatest depth of water to be along the outside of a bend. For the deepest water when rounding the bend in a river, you should navigate your vessel toward the outside of the bend. Also remember, when hugging a bank in a narrow channel, you should take precautions against bank suction, squat, the effects of vessels passing close aboard, clogged sea chests, plugged sea strainers, overheated machinery and striking underwater

obstructions close to the bank. Consider one last thing, if your vessel has grounded on a bar. You should switch to the high suction for condenser circulating water, if it still is submerged.

Clearance Height

New Orleans is a good example of a river port. During low water periods the Mississippi River is only about two feet above Gulf level at New Orleans. During flood stage the river may be 17 to 20 feet above the Gulf. Shipmasters must be aware of the river's height and determine their overhead clearances. Two major collisions with the Huey P. Long Bridge in a brief time span can be attributed to licensed personnel who might have checked clearance height of the bridge more carefully.

Maneuvering in Shallow Water

Squat

Squat occurs when a large vessel is traveling in shallow water and gets sucked down toward the bottom. The faster the vessel travels in shallow water the more dramatic the squat. How does this happen? When your vessel is in shallow water, the water passing between your keel and the seabed travels faster than the surrounding water and pulls your vessel down toward the bottom.

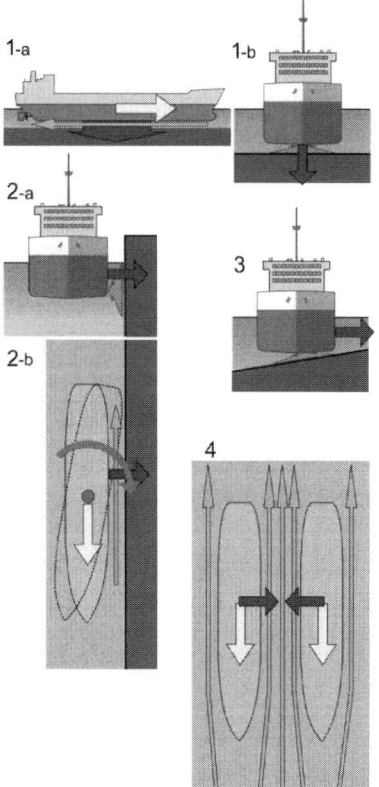

Wikipedia describes it like this "In fluid dynamics, Bernoulli's principle states that an increase in the speed of a fluid occurs simultaneously with a decrease in pressure." The American Practical Navigator has an old school description like this, "For a vessel underway, the bodily sinkage and change of trim which are caused by the pressure distribution on the hull due to the relative motion of the water and the hull. The effect begins to increase significantly at depth to depth ratios of less than 2.5. It increases rapidly with speed and is augmented in narrow channels."

What you need to know about squat to pass quizzes and exams is in the following sentences. Squatting is a shallow water effect that will increase dramatically if you increase your ship's speed past its "critical speed." Your ship is in shallow water and the bow rides up on its bow wave while the stern sinks into a depression of its transverse wave system. This is called squatting. Speed through the water has this effect on a vessel which is underway in shallow water, an increase in speed results in the stern sucking down lower than the bow. A common occurrence when a vessel is running into shallow water is that "squat" will cause a decrease in bottom clearance and an increase in draft.

Interaction with Bank/Passing Ships

Bernoulli's Principle

Bernoulli's Principle states; an increase in the speed of fluid occurs simultaneously with a decrease in pressure. Basically, the principle says that the higher the velocity of the fluid, the lower the pressure. Thus, when you are cruising next to the edge of a channel or another boat your bow is forced away and your stern is sucked in.

Bank Cushion

Bank Cushion forces the bow away from the bank. It is the result of a build up of slower moving water at the bow of a vessel. A vessel traveling down a narrow channel may set off the nearer side due to bank cushion.

Bank Suction

Bank Suction pulls the stern toward the bank. It is the result of faster moving water at the stern of a vessel. A vessel traveling down a narrow channel may have it's stern pulled into nearer side. Remember this can also occur between two vessels passing close to each other. If you happen to be cruising next to your buddies side by side and transferring anything, your bows will pushout and your sterns will suck into each other.

Berthing and Unberthing

As the master of a vessel it is your responsibility to land your vessel at the dock or mooring and leave the dock or mooring safely. Coming to and from the dock or mooring is known as berthing and unberthing. There are a several scenarios the Coast Guard would like you to be familiar with concerning berthing and unberthing.

Berthing

- You are mooring to a buoy. You should approach the buoy with the current form ahead.
- The best time to work a boat into a slip is at slack water.
- Your vessel is a single screw ship with a right-hand propeller. There is no current. The easiest way to make a landing is port side to.
- You are docking a vessel. Wind and current are most favorable when they are parallel to the pier from ahead.

Unberthing

- After casting off moorings at a mooring buoy in calm weather, you should back away a few lengths to clear the buoy and then go ahead on the engines.
- To warp a vessel means to move the vessel by hauling on lines.
- A twin screw can clear the inboard propeller and maneuver off a pier best by holding a(n) forward spring line and going slow ahead on the outboard engine.
- Your vessel is port side to a pier with a spring line lead aft from the bow. In calm weather, putting the engines ahead with the rudder hard left should bring the bow in and the stern out.

Wake Reduction

General

The solution to wake reduction is no mystery. In order to reduce your wake you should reduce your speed. There are a few other point about wakes that are less known. For example, a stream of water immediately surrounding a moving vessel's hull, flowing in the same direction as the vessel is known as wake current. The ratio of the wake speed to the ship's speed is called wake fraction. In addition to a fore and aft motion, wakes have an upward and inward flow.

Anchoring and Mooring

Anchor

An anchor is a device used to secure a ship to the sea floor. It is usually made of metal, attached to a boat by an anchor rode and cast overboard to keep the boat in place by digging into the bottom. A permanent anchor is called a mooring.

The image below shows a variety of different anchor types.

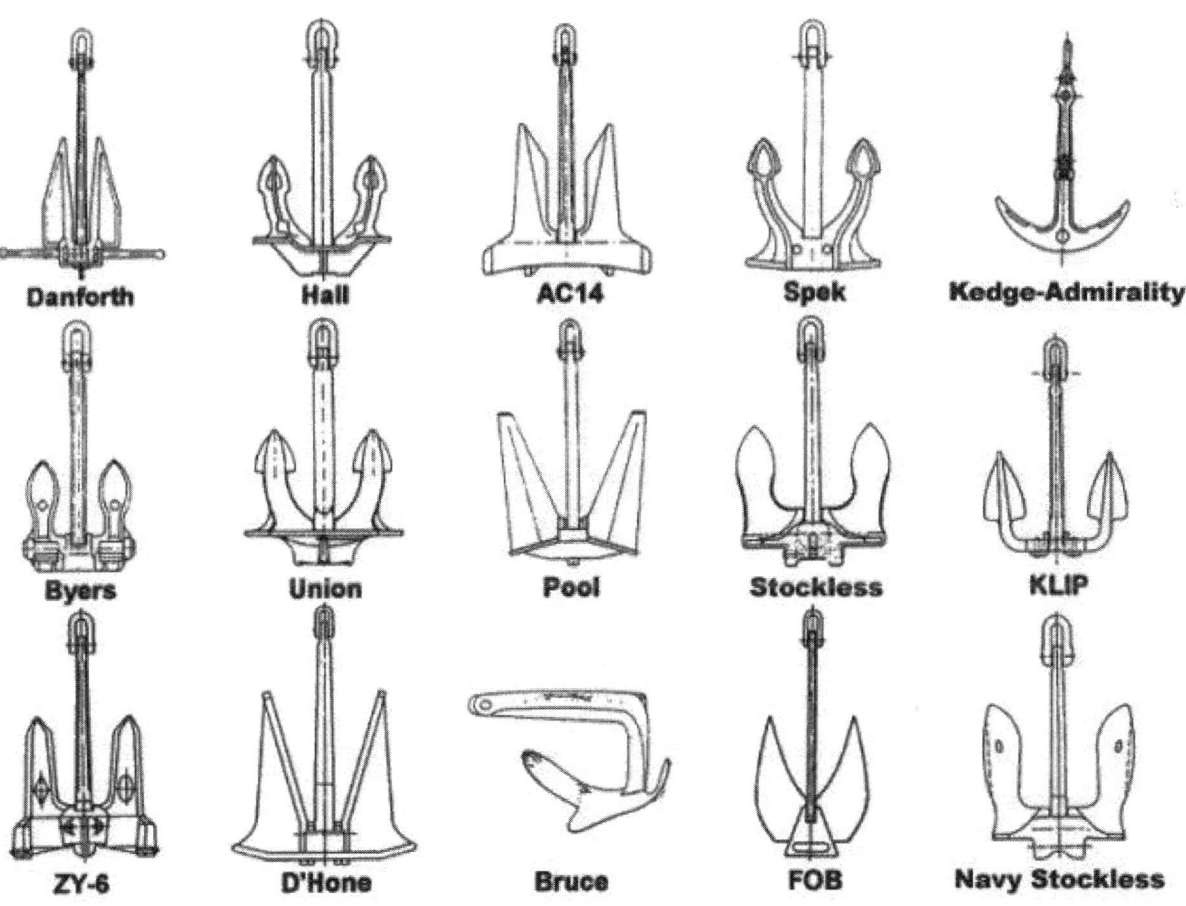

Anchor Anatomy

A Stockless anchor used by larger ship is shown to the right. The basic parts of an anchor are listed below and correspond to the diagram.

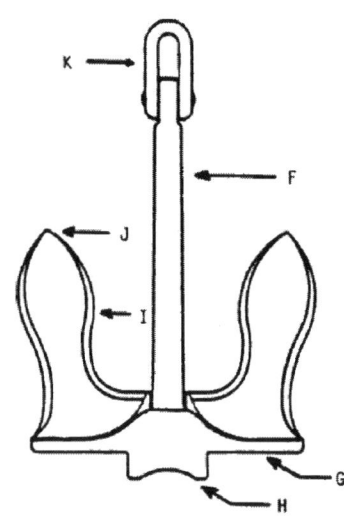

- F. Shank - connects the ring to the body of the anchor
- G. Arm - connects the tripping palm and the flukes
- H. Tripping palm - a tilted surface that causes the flukes to dig into the bottom
- I. Fluke - digs into the bottom and gives the anchor holding power
- J. Bill - point of the fluke that helps the anchor dig in to the bottom
- K. Ring - chain attachment point

Anchor Rode

The anchor rode is the chain or line that connects the anchor to the vessel. The weight of the rode causes it to form a curve called a catenary curve. This curvature acts as a shock absorber between the vessel and the anchor.

Chain is the preferred anchor rode for larger vessels. It is very heavy and creates a large catenary curve which absorbs large shock loads. Three strand nylon is the preferred anchor rode for smaller vessels. It is light, stretchy and easy to handle. When using a light rode it is best to incorporate a length of heavy chain 6 to 10 feet long at the anchor.

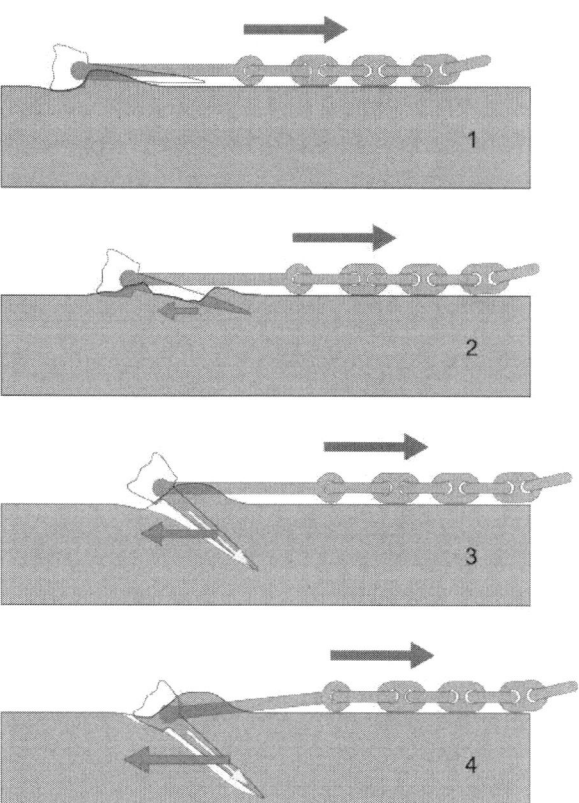

Scope

Scope is the ratio of the length of your anchor rode to the depth of the water. Scope is extremely important in safe anchoring. When anchoring, good practice requires 5 to 7 fathoms of chain for each fathom of depth. In deep water you should use less chain for each fathom of depth. For example, using a scope of five, you should put out 100 feet or rode to anchor in 20 feet of water. The more rode you put out the better your anchor works.

Bottom

The holding capability of an anchor is primarily determined by the anchor's ability to dig in. The angle at which the fluke penetrates the soil is called the tripping angle. Generally speaking, the most favorable bottom for anchoring is a mixture of mud and clay. Conventional anchors are least likely to hold in a bottom consisting of rock.

Dragging

If your vessel is dragging her anchor in a strong wind, you should increase the scope of the anchor rode. The best method of determining if a vessel is dragging anchor is to note changes in bearings of fixed objects onshore. When anchoring in a clay bottom, one hazard that may cause an anchor to drag is the anchor may get shod with clay and not develop full holding power. If you have anchored in a mud and clay bottom and the anchor appears to be dragging in a storm you should drop the second anchor, veer to a good scope, then weigh the first anchor.

Clearing

While anchoring your vessel, the best time to let go the anchor is when the vessel is moving slowly astern over the ground.
Lifting the anchor from the bottom is called weighing the anchor. When a small craft anchor fouls in a rocky bottom, the first attempt to clear it should be made by reversing the angle and direction of the pull, with moderate scope. When weighing anchor in rough sea, you should avoid risk of damaging the bow plate by leaving the anchor underfoot, until the vessel may be brought before the sea.

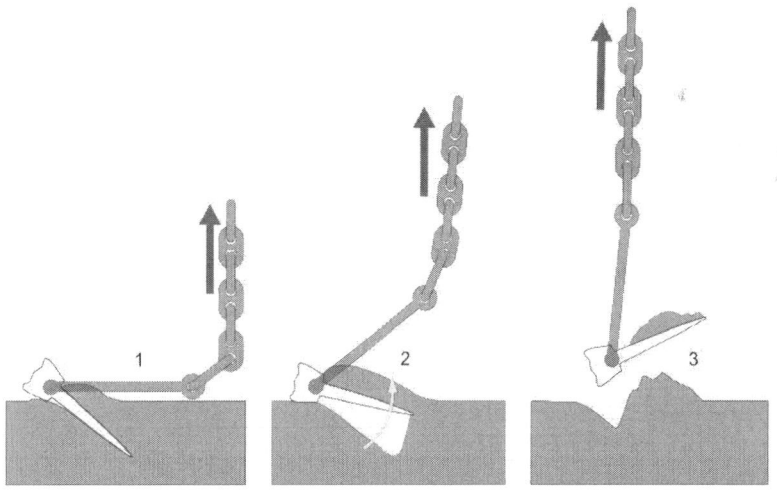

Heavy Weather Operations

General

Heavy weather present many challenges. You may find that your vessels bow pounds on the waves, your propeller lifts clear out of the water or, worst case scenario your vessel surfs down a wave yaws to one side and broaches leaving it in danger of capsizing. Whatever happens keep calm and remember the following examples to do well on quizzes and your final exam.

You are steaming in a heavy gale and find it necessary to heave to. Under most circumstances, it is best done by taking the seas fine on the bow and reducing the speed to the minimum to hold that position. When making way in heavy seas you notice your vessel's screw is being lifted clear of the water and racing. One way to correct this would be to decrease your speed. You are underway in heavy weather and your bow is into the seas. To prevent pounding, you should decrease speed. When a boat turns broadside to heavy seas and winds, thus exposing the boat to the dangers of capsizing, the boat has broached.

Motion

When handling a vessel in heavy weather there are six motions you will encounter. These motions are divided into two types, translations and rotation.

Translations

- Heave - up-and-down motion caused by the vertical component of wave motion.
- Sway - side-to-side motion caused by the horizontal component of wave motion.
- Surge - fore-and-aft motion caused by the horizontal component of wave motion

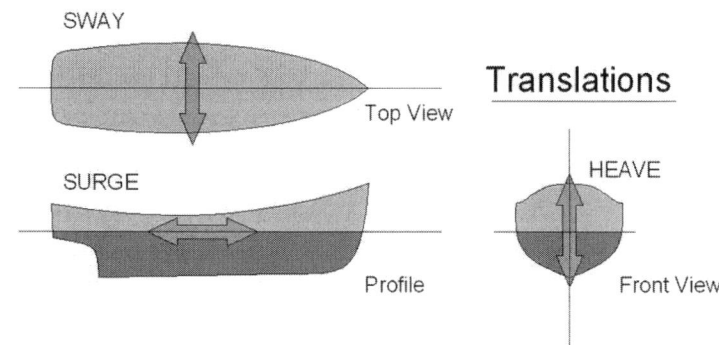

Rotations

- Roll - side-to-side rotational motion about the longitudinal axis of the vessel. Rhythmic motion most pronounced when the vessel is taking waves on the beam. Taking the waves on the bow or stern quarter can lessen the motion.

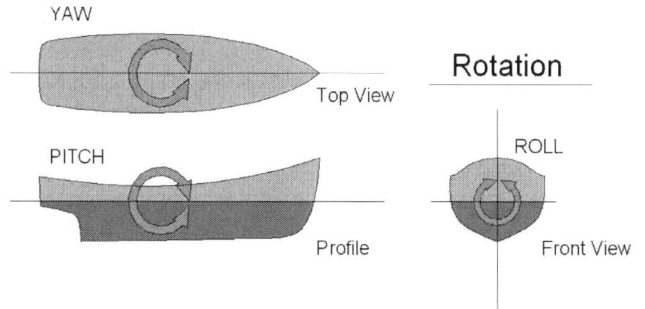

165

- Pitch - sometimes called hobby horsing. Motion about the transverse axis of the vessel. The vessel pounds through the waves. Slowing or taking the waves at more of an angle can help to decrease the pitching.
- Yaw - turning about a vertical axis, usually close to the bow. The stern is pushed from side to side by following seas. It can be lessened by increasing speed, by shifting weight to the stern, and by taking seas on the quarter rather than dead astern.

General: Turning Circle, Pivot Point, Advance and Transfer

Each vessel has unique characteristics when she is maneuvering. When precise piloting is necessary in an area with limited maneuvering space, when approaching an anchorage, or when operating close to other vessels, you must always consider your vessel's turning characteristics.

Turning Circle

The turning circle of a vessel making a turn over 360 degrees is the path followed by the center of gravity. The distance a vessel moves at right angles to the original course, when a turn of 180° has been completed, is called the tactical diameter. The final diameter is the diameter of a circle your vessel traverses after turning through 360° while maintaining the same speed and rudder angle. The final diameter is always less than the tactical diameter. The image on the right illustrate tactical ane final diameters.

Pivot Point

The pivoting point of a vessel going ahead is about one-third of the vessel's length from the bow. When underway and proceeding ahead, as the speed increases, the pivot point tends to move forward. When backing down with sternway, the pivot point of a vessel is about one-quarter of the vessel's length from the stern. The effect of wind on exposed areas of the vessel is most noticeable when backing.

Advance

The distance a vessel moves parallel to the original course from the point where the rudder is put over to any point on the turning circle is called the advance.

166

Transfer

The distance a vessel moves perpendicular to the original course from the point where the rudder is put over to any point on the turning circle is called the transfer.

The amount of advance and transfer for a given vessel depends primarily upon the amount of rudder you use and the angle through which the vessel is to be turned. The speed of the vessel has little effect. The figure at right is a simplified illustration of advance and transfer for a turn that is less than 90°.

On ships advance and transfer is plotted for turns in confined waters to determine critical turning points. From the vessel's operating characteristics, a table can be constructed to indicate the distance from the point where the rudder is put over to the intersection with any new course line for various course alterations, speeds, and rudder angles.

Head Reach

Headreach is distance the vessel travels between taking action to stop her and being stationary in the water.

Vessel Power Plant

Small Engine Operations and Maintenance

Rudder

For the rudder to work you must have a flow of water around it. If there is no moving water, or the water is turbulent, the rudder's effectiveness is greatly reduced. The rudder is also designed to work most efficiently when the vessel is going forward. The effectiveness of the rudder when the vessel is backing is dramatically reduced.

Propeller

The propeller's main function is to push the vessel forward through the water and is optimized to do just that. Backing is secondary and the propeller is less effective. When talking about propellers there are several important factors.

Right-Hand and Left-Hand Propeller

Is a propeller Right-hand or Left-hand rotating? This is determined by viewing the vessel from astern. If the propeller is rotating clockwise for the vessel to move forward it is called a Right-hand propeller. A counterclockwise rotation would be a Left-hand propeller. Most single propeller or "single screw" vessels are equipped with Right-hand propellers.

Pitch

Pitch is the "twist" in the propeller blades. Pitch is measured in terms of the distance the vessel will move forward during one revolution of the propeller. A 12 inch pitch would mean the vessel will travel 12 inches during one revolution. A 60 inch pitch would mean the vessel will move 60 inches during one revolution. In reality propellers are not 100% efficient so the vessel would actually travel less distance. This loss is called slip.

Sidewise Force Prop Walk

When a propeller spins it pushes on the water and the water pushes back causing the vessel to move forward. In addition to pushing the vessel forward the spinning propeller pushes the stern of the vessel sidewise. This sidewise force is called prop walk and on some single screw vessels it makes backing under control nearly impossible.

The sidewise force is due to the sidewise push of the top propeller blade being less than the sidewise push of the bottom propeller blade. The sidewise force pushes in the direction of the top propeller blade. A Right-hand prop will walk to starboard in forward and walk to port in reverse. A left hand prop will do the opposite.

Single Screw

There are a couple of things to remember about the behavior of single screw vessels. First thing to remember is that single screw vessels will have either a right-hand or left-hand propeller. When you back a right-handed single screw vessel it backs to port and the bow falls off to starboard. In order to back a right-handed, single-screw vessel in a straight line, you will probably need to use some right rudder. Vessels that have a left-hand propeller will have opposite handling characteristics.

Twin Screw

A twin-screw vessel has an advantage over a single-screw ship because side forces will be eliminated and each propeller can be used independently to control the vessel more accurately. The following sentences about the behavior of twin screwed vessels demonstrates the intuitive nature of handling them and come in handy when taking quizzes and exams.

If you are conning a twin-screw vessel going ahead with rudders amidships and the port screw stops turning the bow will go to port. If you are conning a twin-screw vessel going astern with rudders amidships and the port screw stops turning the bow will go to starboard. With rudders amidships and negligible wind, a twin-screw vessel moving astern with both engines backing will back in a fairly straight line. The best way to steer a twin-screw vessel if you lose your rudder is by using one engine running at reduced speed and controlling the vessel with the other.

Engine Maintenance

Checklist

Running through a maintenance checklist is a good idea to keep your vessels engines in good condition. The daily checks and maintenance varies from engine to engine. Examples of checklist items are below:
- Check engine oil level and condition, look for metal shavings
- Check transmission fluid level and condition, look for metal shavings
- Inspect racor and drain excess water
- Inspect fuel line for cracks and leaks
- Inspect water intake lines for cracks and leaks
- Inspect exhaust bellows for cracks and leaks
- Inspect air filter for debris and moisture
- Look for any drips, metal shavings, loose bolts and scorch marks in the engine room

Best Practices

There are couple things captain's may do to keep a record of past maintenance. Keep a log book on the boat and record all maintenance in the log. Everytime any filter is changed mark the date it was changed directly on the filter with a sharpe.

Maritime Law

National Maritime Law

Certification and Documentation of Vessels

Certificate of Inspection (COI)

All small passenger vessels that carry more than six passengers need a COI to operate. The inspection is done by the US Coast Guard. Below is an outline of important aspects of the inspection for COI.

- All commercial vessels less than 100 gross tons carrying more than six passengers, including at least one passenger for hire, must be inspected and certificated (issued a Certificate of Inspection) by the Coast Guard.
- The inspection and certification process normally commences before vessel construction starts. Plans showing the hull, machinery, electrical, fuel, and other arrangements must be submitted to the Coast Guard for approval.
- During construction, Coast Guard inspectors make frequent visits to ensure construction is in accordance with the approved plans.
- When construction is completed, sea trials are conducted, and firefighting and lifesaving equipment are examined to ensure proper outfitting.
- The Master and Mate of small passenger vessels are licensed by the Coast Guard. They must document their experience and pass a written and physical examination
- Inspections of the vessel and its equipment continue throughout its life.
- At routine dry-dock inspections, the underwater body is surveyed along with its fastenings, sea valves, tail shaft, and other thru-hull fittings.

Vessel Documentation

Vessel Documentation is different than a Certificate of Inspection. Any vessel over 5 GRT can be documented.

Vessel documentation is a national form of registration. It is one of the oldest functions of Government, dating back to the 11th Act of the First Congress. Documentation provides conclusive evidence of nationality for international purposes, provides for unhindered commerce between the states, and admits vessels to certain restricted trades, such as coastwise trade and the fisheries. Since 1920, vessel financing has been enhanced through the availability of preferred mortgages on documented vessels.

Pollution Prevention Regulations

Pollution is covered by two sets of rules first is the International Convention for the Prevention of Pollution from Ships, 1973 (amended in 1978) or commonly known as MARPOL(73/78). The second is 33 CFR Subchapter O which covers pollution.

Oil

Any discharge of oil is illegal and must be reported to the USCG. In the case of a spill the following steps should be taken:
- Stop the discharge.
- Notify the USCG.
- Prevent spreading and remove as much as possible.
  - containment (booms)
  - mechanical (skimmers)
  - absorbents (straw or reclaimed fibers)

Sewage

On a ship the "head" or "toilet" is a Marine Sanitation Device (MSD). MSD's includes any equipment for installation on board a vessel which is designed to receive, retain, treat, or discharge sewage, and any process to treat such sewage. Sewage means human body wastes and the wastes from toilets and other receptacles intended to receive or retain body waste.

Plastic and Garbage

Garbage includes food wastes, glass, metal, crockery, rags, and paper. Note that "garbage" does not include plastics. Plastics are prohibited from being discharged anywhere in the world, at any time.

Discharge

Discharge is the intentional or unintentional emission; includes spilling, leaking, pumping, pouring, emptying, or dumping. The regulations for what may be discharged from vessels are determined by miles offshore.
- Within 3 miles - dishwater or greywater. This includes dishwasher, shower, bath, washbasin, and laundry drainage. Does not include drainage from toilets, urinals, hospital, or cargo spaces.
- Between 3 and 12 Miles - the above plus glass, metal, crockery, bottles, food waste, paper, rags, dunnage (all ground to less than one inch), and toilets.
- Between 12 and 25 miles - the above even if not ground but not including garbage that floats or dunnage.
- 25 miles or more - the above plus floating garbage and dunnage.

Credentialing of Seaman

Shipment and Discharge, Manning

Operator of Uninspected Passenger Vessels are required to keeps their Coast Guard License aboard only when carrying passengers for hire. Total responsibility for shipping and discharging the seaman is that of the Master of the vessel. The Master of the vessel is responsible for properly manning a vessel in accordance with all applicable laws, regulations and international conventions.The Certificate of Inspection shows the minimum required crew a vessel must have to navigate from one port in the United States to another.

Shipboard Management and Training

Sanitation

Potable Water

Potable water is water that is safe to drink or to use for food preparation. To insure the flow of safe water from outlets used for drinking and culinary purposes on a vessel, it is necessary first to load or manufacture water of drinking water quality. Next, the sanitation facilities built into the vessel must be utilized in a manner which prevents contamination of the water during normal ship operations.

Source of Potable Water

In ports of the United States and its possessions potable water for vessels should be obtained only from water supplies and at watering points (including water boats) approved by the Surgeon General of the Public Health Service.

Filling Hose

A separate hose should be kept on each vessel and used only for loading potable water. Under no circumstances should non-potable liquids pass through it. If there is a hose at the pier where potable water is loaded, none need be kept on the vessel. The hose should be handled so that the ends are not dragged through or accidentally dropped into contaminated water, or otherwise contaminated.

Filling Hose Stowage

The potable water hose and such hydrant adapters as may be required should be stowed in a closed cabinet, on a rack or reel, or hung on brackets and located near the vessel's filling line connection, preferably on the bulkhead adjacent to the filling line connection so it will be easily accessible at all times. This will minimize the possibility of crewmembers using another hose, one which might be contaminated. These facilities should be installed at least 18 inches above the deck.

Disinfection of Potable Water System

Any portion of the potable water system which has been repaired, contains replacements, or has been contaminated, should be cleaned, disinfected, and flushed before the affected units are placed in operation as a part of the system, or whenever the system otherwise has become contaminated. Chlorine compounds used for disinfecting potable water systems are chlorinated lime, high-test hypochlorite (HTH), perchloron, pittchlor or their equivalent, or commercially prepared liquid sodium hypochlorite such as clorox, zonite, or their equivalent.

Rodent Control

Rats and mice manage to gain access to vessels despite numerous safeguards, it is necessary to adopt control measures to combat them. Keeping down or eliminating the rodent population on a vessel may involve the use of poisons and traps. Most rodenticides are toxic to humans; therefore you should follow instructions as to their use carefully.

Ships Business

Licensing Requirements

Station License

- Recreational Vessels
  - o Do not require a station license when equipped with a VHF radio, Radar or EPIRB if operated in Domestic waters.
  - o Station licenses are required on recreational boats if:
    - 65 feet or longer.
    - Travel includes foreign ports.
    - Equipped with single sideband radios.
- Commercial Vessels
  - Must have a station license because they are required to have a VHF radio aboard.
  - Some commercial vessels may require a certificate of compliance from the FCC
- All forms and Fees are regulated by the FCC.

Operator Licensing

- Recreational Vessels
  - No operator's license is required if you do not:
    - Enter a foreign port
    - Do not have a single sideband radio
  - Must have a "Restricted Radio Operator's Permit: if
    - They travel to foreign ports
    - Have a SSB Radio with an output of 100 watts or less of power.
- Commercial Vessels
  - Commercial vessels carrying 6 or less passengers are required to have a "Restricted Radio Operators Permit if they:
- Travel to foreign ports.
    - Have a SSB Radio with an output of 100 watts or less of power.

Marine Radio Operators Permit

- Vessels sailing the Great Lakes over 65 feet.
- Towing another vessel over 65 feet in length in the Great Lakes.
- SSB radio has an output that is greater than 100 watts.
- Land based station.
- All vessels over 6 passengers for hire.
- All vessels requiring a Certificate of Compliance.
- All vessels 100 gross tons and over carrying (1) one passenger for hire.
- Every towing vessel over 26 feet.
- Every dredge and floating plant.

Radio logs are required on every inspected vessel. The radio log must list the hours of operation, operating condition of the radio, any radio checks performed, all radio tests and maintenance performed by a licensed radio technician, all MAYDAY messages received and all MAYDAY, PAN — PAN or SECURITE' messages sent.

Entries in the log may never be erased. If a change is required, the error should be crossed out and accompanied by the initials of the person making the correction. This is true of all logs on a vessel.

Helpful Tip

Be sure to read the Ship's Business Statements to Recognize. They will help you do well on all quizzes and exams covering Ship's Business.

Fire Prevention and Firefighting Appliances

Basic Firefighting and Prevention

Prevention

The best way to fight a fire is to prevent it from starting. The following points aid in the prevention of fires. Small quantities of flammable liquids needed at a work site should be in a metal container with a tight cap. Spontaneous ignition can result from careless disposal or storage of material. A chemical additive to LPG (Liquid Propane Gas) gives it a characteristic odor if you smell it ventilate the area. Storage batteries should be charged in a well ventilated area because they emit hydrogen.

Spread

Once a fire starts it may spread rapidly. The spread of fire is prevented by removing combustibles from the endangered area. To prevent the spread of fire by convection you should close all openings to the area. A fire in the galley always poses the additional threat of a grease fire in the ventilation system. If you are underway when a fire breaks out in the forward part of your vessel you should put the vessel's stern into the wind.

Electrical

Danger of shock to personnel is the most important consideration when determining how to fight an electrical fire. Another important step in fighting any electrical fire is to de-energize the circuit. If you are fighting a fire in the electrical switchboard in the engine room, you should secure the power and use a portable CO_2 extinguisher. If you use dry chemicals to fight an electrical fire they should be aimed at the source of the flame.

Classes of Fire

A, B, C, D and K

Class A fire is in paper, wood, cloth, trash and other common materials.
Class B fire is in gasoline, oil, paint and other flammable liquids.
Class C fire is in live electrical equipment.
Class D fire is in metal and metal alloys.
Class K fire is in cooking media, vegetable oil, animal fats and oils.

CLASSES OF FIRES	TYPES OF FIRES	PICTURE SYMBOL
A	Wood, paper, cloth, trash & other ordinary materials.	
B	Gasoline, oil, paint and other flammable liquids.	
C	May be used on fires involving live electrical equipment without danger to the operator.	
D	Combustible metals and combustible metal alloys.	
K	Cooking media (Vegetable or Animal Oils and Fats)	

Chemistry of Fire

Fire Triangle

The fire triangle is a diagram for understanding the necessary ingredients for most fires. The three components are:

1. Fuel
2. Heat
3. Oxygen

To control or extinguish an ordinary fire eliminate any of its three components. The fire triangle will collapse and the fire will go out. For example, if heat can be removed by cooling the fuel to a temperature below its ignition point with water the fire can no longer exist.

Remove Fuel

Take all possible measures to prevent additional fuel from reaching the fire.

Remove Heat

Removing heat is accomplished by using water and water sprays. Foam smothers a fire and has a secondary cooling effect.

Remove Oxygen

Oxygen can be kept out of cargo holds by closing all openings to the atmosphere and stopping forced ventilation. Once ventilation to the hold is at a minimum the hold may be flooded with CO_2 in order to remove oxygen. A hold may also be flooded by foam which removes oxygen from a fire by covering it with a layer of carbon dioxide bubbles that do not let oxygen pass through.

Emergency Procedures

Passenger and Crew Safety in Emergencies

Communication

Use the VHF radiotelephone calling/safety/distress frequency is 156.8 MHz (channel 16) when reporting a emergency situation to the USCG and vessels near you. The three radio emergency signals are:

- Mayday is the distress signal and means your vessel is sinking or on fire and you can no longer stay on it.
- Pan-Pan is the urgency signal and usually means you need help but are not in danger. For example, a crewman is severely injured and needs to be airlifted from the vessel.
- Securite is the safety signal to announce a storm warning, danger to navigation, or special aid to navigation.

Drills

Drills have an important role in keeping passengers and crew safe in emergencies. Carry out all drills as if the emergency is actually taking place and practice them monthly. Be familiar with the following points:

- A new crew member aboard your fishing vessel, who has not received any safety instructions or participated in any drills, reports on board. The Master must provide a safety orientation before sailing.
- Recovering an individual from the water emergency is required to be covered at the required periodic drills on a fishing vessel.
- Coast Guard regulations require that all of the following emergencies be covered at the periodic drills on a fishing vessel EXCEPT emergency towing.
- While reading the muster list you see that "3 short blasts on the whistle and 3 short rings of the bell" is the signal for dismissal from fire and emergency stations.

Muster List

A muster list provides crew members with a plan to manage emergency situations. It gives clear instructions to be followed in the event of an emergency for every person on board and ensures that all vital duties are assigned. Another term for muster list is station bill. Below is an example muster list.

SMALL PASSENGER VESSEL MUSTER LIST

[NAME OF VESSEL]   [MASTER'S SIGNATURE]

EMERGENCY SIGNALS

Fire and Emergency: A continuous sounding of the ship's whistle supplemented by a continuous ringing of the General Alarm bells for not less than 10 seconds.

Dismissal from Fire and Emergency Stations: 3 short blasts on the whistle and 3 short rings on the General Alarm bells.

Abandon Ship: 7 short blasts and 1 long blast on the ship's whistle and the same signal on the General Alarm bells.

Dismissal from Boat Stations: 3 short blasts on the whistle.

Man Overboard: Immediately throw a ring life buoy. Hail, and pass the word "MAN OVERBOARD - PORT (OR STARBOARD) SIDE" to the pilothouse, which sounds the international signal "O" (— — —) at least four times on the ship's whistle followed by the same signal on the General Alarm bells.

FIRE AND EMERGENCY INSTRUCTIONS

1. If you discover a fire, immediately notify the pilothouse and fight the fire with suitable available equipment.

2. As soon as you hear the Fire and Emergency signal, start all fire pumps. Close all watertight doors, hatches and air ports. Stop all fans, blowers and heating, air conditioning or ventilating equipment. Lead a fire hose out in the affected area as directed.

3. When you hear the hail or signal for a "Man Overboard" throw a ring life buoy overboard. Stop the engines. Keep the person and/or the ring life buoy in sight. Maneuver the vessel. Prepare to recover the man overboard.

ABANDON SHIP INSTRUCTIONS

1. When handling signals sound on the ship's whistle these signals mean:

   (-) One short blast means to launch the inflatable liferaft(s) and/or rescue boat.

   (- -) Two short blasts means to stop the launching procedure.

2. The Master may alter assignments in emergencies to fit actual conditions.

RESPONSIBILITIES

1. These instructions apply to each and every person aboard this vessel. 2. As soon as you board this vessel you must learn where your assigned fire and emergency station is and become thoroughly familiar with your duties in all emergencies. As a

"Passenger" (including any other person on this vessel in addition to the crew), you must ask and expect to be shown your liferaft station before the vessel sails.

3. Each crewmember and "passenger" must take part in all emergency drills and be appropriately dressed to do so. This includes donning a lifejacket or immersion suit correctly.

4. The Deck Hand#2 (#6) or a designated seaman must: 1) warn passengers of any danger to themselves or to the vessel; 2) see that passengers dress appropriately and correctly don their lifejackets and/or immersion suits; 3) assemble and direct passengers to their emergency stations; 4) keep order in passageways and on stairways; 5) control passenger movements; 6) gather and move a supply of blankets to each inflatable liferaft.

5. The chain of command appears in descending order in the # column with the Master at the top. If a key person becomes disabled, the next senior member (i.e., the person higher on the list) assumes his/her place and his/her duties.

6. The Mate is responsible for the maintenance and readiness of all lifesaving and firefighting appliances and equipment on and above the main deck. The Able Seaman #1 is responsible for the readiness of all lifesaving and firefighting appliances and equipment below the main deck.

7. During periods of restricted visibility, you must keep all watertight doors and ports below or leading to the main deck closed and dogged except any openings specifically exempted by the Master.

#	RATING	FIRE &. EMERGENCY STATIONS	ABANDON SHIP - BOAT STATIONS
1.	MASTER	Commands from the pilothouse. Operates all controls, radios and public address system. Directs and supervises all operations. Instructs the crew on specific duties according to circumstances. Assigns two crewmen to man the rescue boat. Orders man overboard drills.	Stationed on deck at liferaft #1. Musters crew. Directs all operations. If passengers (etc.) are on board, sees they board assigned liferafts. Takes command of liferaft #1.
2.	MATE	At the scene of the emergency. Provides fire extinguishing or emergency equipment as needed. Closes ports, watertight doors and air ducts for actual fire and for all drills.	Stationed in command of liferaft #2. Removes, checks, and activates EPIRB as ordered or when conditions warrant.
3.	ABLE SEAMAN #1	Stands by in engine room at or near telephone or escape hatch. Start pumps. Stops blowers. Closes all watertight doors and other closures.	Stationed on deck at liferaft #1. Assists in launching and is second in command of liferaft.
4.	ABLE SEAMAN #2	Leads out fire hose #1. Opens valve, charges hose, and tends the nozzle. On the Master's orders, he reports to the scene of the emergency.	Stationed on deck at liferaft #2. On orders, he assists in launching the liferaft and assists assigned passengers to board liferaft #2 before boarding. Is second in command.
5.	Deck Hand #1	Leads out fire hose #2. Opens valve, charges hose, and tends the nozzle. On the Master's orders he reports to the scene of the emergency.	Stationed on deck at liferaft #1. On orders, he assists in launching liferaft #1. Assists assigned passengers to board this liferaft before boarding himself.
6.	Deck Hand #2	Stops ventilation system for the galley and accommodation spaces. Arouses all passengers. Checks for adequate dress and properly donned lifejackets. Evacuates and secures the quarters. Reports to his/her abandon ship station and stands by awaiting 's orders.	Stationed on deck at liferaft #2 - on Master's orders assists in launching liferaft #2. Assists assigned passengers to board this liferaft and then boards himself.

Man Overboard Procedures

General

A Man Overboard situation is one in which someone has fallen overboard. The key to rescuing a man overboard are well-conducted drills. A person who sees someone fall overboard should call for help and keep the individual in sight. On a small boat, if someone fell overboard and you did not know over which side the person fell, you should stop the propellers from turning and throw a ring buoy over the side.

Watch

You are standing the wheel watch when you hear the cry, "Man overboard starboard side". You should instinctively give full right rudder. This action moves the propelles away from the person in the water. If someone falls over the port side you would give left full rudder to move the propellers away from the person in the water. On very large vessels it is faster to deploy a lifeboat to get the person in the water. Remember, if the person appears in danger of drowning, the lifeboat should make the most direct approach.

Anyone sighting a man fall overboard must shout in their loudest voice, "Man Overboard Port Side," (or starboard side) and then repeat the call as many times as is necessary until it is obvious that the helmsman is taking the necessary actions. A life ring or PFD should be thrown over to the person in the water. One person is assigned the task of keeping the person in sight while the appropriate turn is made by the helmsman.

Timing

Recovering a man in the water is a problem for most vessels, large or small. Large ships require a great deal of space and time to maneuver simply to return to the spot where a person fell overboard. Sometimes, especially in a narrow channel, the space simply is not available to make a turn. Cold water may limit recovery time to a few brief minutes so every second counts.

Consider three situations:
- Immediate - The watch officer sees or hears the man fall overboard and maneuvers the vessel at once and without delay.
- Delayed - An eyewitness reports the casualty to the bridge but action starts after this or some other delay.
- Missing person - Nobody sees the person fall overboard or knows exactly when it occurred.

Turns

A large vessel moving ahead at full speed may perform four basic maneuvers to return close enough to the man overboard to permit recovery. The choice of maneuver to use depends on the time factor involved and the type of vessel. These four maneuvers are:
1. Single Turn
2. Race Track Turn
3. Williamson Turn
4. Scharnow Turn

Single Turn

The single turn is useful on small vessels is immediate situations. It is the fastest way to return to the person in the water. The diagram shows that you approach the site at right angles to your original course.

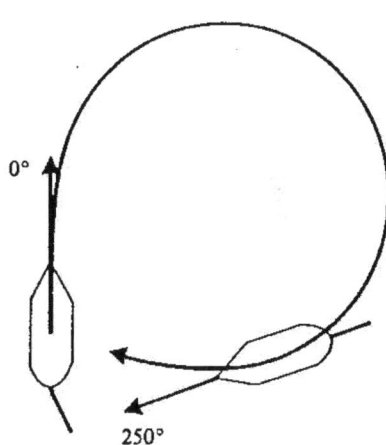

To make the Single Turn, follow these steps:
1. Order the rudder hard over toward the side the person fell over.
2. Return the rudder to a midships position at the point where your vessel has turned through an arc of 250° or almost three-quarters of a complete circle.
3. Slow and prepare to stop the vessel.

Race Track Turn

The Racetrack turn is also called the two turn approach. Although it is a slower than the single turn, its straight final approach leg helps you calculate your approach to the victim in the water accurately. Primarily used in good visibility and in an immediate situation, a large vessel will return to the victim in the water even when they are temporarily lost from view.

To make the Race Track Turn follow these steps:
1. X marks where the person falls overboard.
2. Place the rudder hard over toward the side where the person fell overboard.
3. When clear of the person, go full ahead on your engine(s) with full rudder until you reach the reciprocal of your original course.
4. Steady your rudder on the reciprocal course for a sufficient distance that will allow you to make a desirable straight final approach.
5. Use full rudder to turn toward the person in the water.

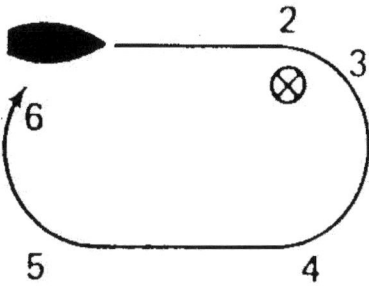

6. Steady on your original course and make your approach the person in the water.

Williamson Turn

The Williamson turn is suitable for both immediate and delayed action situations. Your final approach to the person in the water is at 180° to your original course. A Williamson turn will carry the vessel further from the scene than a Single Turn but it will return the vessel to the person in the water with a greater degree of certainty. This is a significant factor in reduced visibility or in cases involving very large turning circles where you may lose sight of the person in the water.

To perform the Williamson turn:
1. Put the rudder hard over to the side on which the person fell in the water.
2. Hold the rudder hard over until your vessel begins to swing and steady up on a course that is only 60° off your original course.
3. With the vessel steady on this new course, swing the rudder hard over to the other side. Hold it there until the vessel is on a reciprocal course that is 180° from your original course.
4. Maintain your original speed until the vessel is steady on the reciprocal course.
5. All hands must search for the person in the water. Keep him in view. Prepare to recover him as ordered.

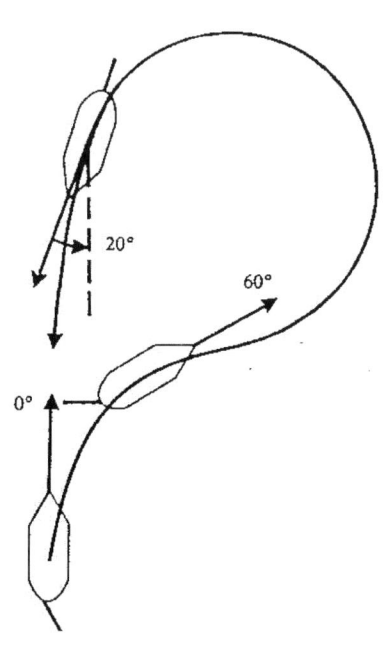

Scharnow Turn

The Scharnow turn is not appropriate in an immediate action situation. Like the Williamson turn, it returns your vessel to a reciprocal course.

To make a Scharnow Turn:
1. Put the rudder hard over to the side on which the person fell in the water.
2. Put the rudder hard over to the other side at the point where your vessel has turned through an arc of 240°.
3. When heading 20° short of a reciprocal course, return the rudder to a midships position so the vessel will turn to the reciprocal course.

Both the Scharnow turn and the Williamson turn will return a vessel to a reciprocal course and are suitable

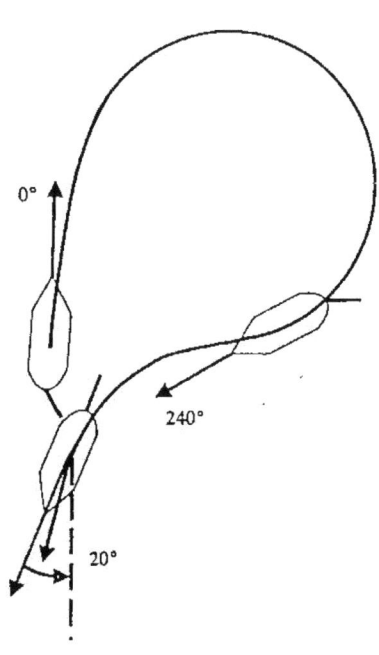

for missing person situations. The Scharnow turn is faster than the Williamson turn. However, it is significant to note that when you perform a Williamson Turn, the man overboard is ahead of you at the end of your turn. Using the Scharnow Turn the man overboard is behind you at the end of the turn. Consequently it is not the proper turn for immediate action cases.

If the MOB is not immediately recovered, notify the Coast Guard and all vessels in the vicinity by radiotelephone or VHF. Standard man overboard turns do not guarantee to return your vessel to an exact reciprocal course. You may not run down your own wake without considerable practice. Therefore, you should practice these turns in man overboard drills to allow for the particular characteristics of your vessel and the effects of environmental conditions on the vessel and the person in the water.

Abandon Ship Procedures

Abandon ship is your worst case scenario. Remember to stick with your ship as long as it sticks with you. Only abandon ship when your immersion suit or life raft has become a better shelter than your ship.

General

If passengers are onboard your vessel when an abandon ship drill is carried out they should take part. After abandoning ship everyone should remain together in the vessel's last known position. If you reach shore in a life raft, the first thing to do is drag the raft ashore and lash it down for a shelter.

Abandon Ship Training and Drills

Material for abandon-ship training must be aboard each vessel. It must contain instructions and information about the lifesaving appliances aboard the vessel and about the best methods of survival. Any crew member excused from an abandon-ship drill must participate in the next one, so that each member participates in at least one each month. As far as practicable, each abandon-ship drill must be conducted as if there were an actual emergency.

Collision

Damage Control

A vessel is described as a two compartment vessel when it will float if any two adjacent compartments are flooded. A vessel of not more than 65 feet in length must have a collision bulkhead if it carries more than 49 passengers.

In plugging submerged holes; rags, wedges, and other materials should be used in conjunction with plugs to reduce the water leaking around the plugs. When plugging holes below the waterline you should reduce the entry of water as much as possible.

Temporary Repairs

General

Hull damage at or just above the waterline should be repaired first. Repairing damage to the hull at or above the waterline reduces the threat of continued progressive downflooding. A crack in the deck plating of a vessel may be temporarily prevented from increasing in length by drilling a hole at each end of the crack. The objective of shoring a damaged bulkhead is to support and hold the damaged area in the damaged position.

Fire Explosion

General

Traditionally the signal for fire and emergency is the ship's whistle sounding for over 10 seconds. You should be most concerned about a possible explosion or fire in fuel tanks during fueling when fuel first strikes the tank bottom. Wind affects the spread of fire and the crews ability to fight it. Remember, if you are underway when a fire breaks out in the forward part of your vessel, you should put the vessel's stern into the wind. If there is a fire aft aboard your vessel, you should head the bow into the wind and decrease speed.

Emergency Towing

General

In some situations you may need to tow another vessel in order to give assistance.
If a tug is approaching a broken down vessel to take it in tow in moderately heavy weather it should approach from downwind in most cases. When a vessel is brought alongside it should be fended off the towing vessel by fenders. The biggest problem you generally encounter when towing a single tow astern yaw. An effective way to stop excessive yaw of the vessel being towed is to move weight to the stern. The greatest danger of an overriding tow is collision between the tow and the stern of the towing vessel.

Lifesaving

Survival at Sea

CPR

General

CPR is an emergency procedure that combines chest compressions often with artificial ventilation in an effort to manually preserve intact brain function until further measures are taken to restore spontaneous blood circulation and breathing in a person who is in cardiac arrest. The MOST important element in administering CPR is starting the treatment quickly. Before CPR is started, you should establish an open airway. When starting CPR on a drowning victim, you should begin mouth-to-mouth ventilation as soon as possible.

First Aid

Bleeding

In all but the most severe cases, bleeding from a wound should be controlled by applying direct pressure to the wound. Once bleeding has been controlled by using a sterile dressing and direct pressure, you should apply a pressure bandage over the dressing. A tourniquet should be used to control bleeding ONLY when all other means have failed.

Burns

First degree burn

There is a reddening of the skin but no other apparent damage. For small, first-degree burns the quickest method to relieve pain is to immerse the burn in cold water.

Second degree burn

There is reddening of the skin, blistering, and swelling. The proper treatment for this injury is to immerse the arm in cold water for 1 to 2 hours, apply burn ointment, and bandage.

Third degree burn

There is extensive damage to the skin with charring present. When treating a person for third degree burns, you should cover the burns with thick, sterile dressings.

Breaks

A person suffering from possible broken bones and internal injuries should not be moved but made comfortable until medical assistance arrives. You should FIRST treat a simple fracture by preventing further movement of the bone. A compound fracture is a fracture in which the bone may be visible and it is the most serious type of fracture is compound.

Life Saving Appliance Operations for T-Boats

Life Jacket

PFD stands for Personal Flotation Device. Type I personal flotation devices are designed to turn an unconscious person's face clear of the water. Kapok life jackets should NOT be stowed near open flame or where smoking is permitted, used as seats, pillows, or foot rests or left on open decks. Life jackets which are severely damaged should be replaced.

Deck General/Safety
Statements to Recognize

Seamanship

Marlinespike Seamanship

Ropes and Lines

1. Marline spike seamanship can be defined as **the set of processes and skills used to make, repair, and use rope.**
2. The set of processes and skills used to make, repair, and use rope is **Marlinspike seamanship.**
3. A rope is **a length of fibers, twisted or braided together.**
    a. Cut to length to serve a specific purpose.
4. A line is **rope cut to a specific length to serve a specific purpose.**

Chafing Gear

5. Chafing gear is normally used **on mooring lines.**
6. Chafing gear **reduces and prevents wear caused by the rubbing of one object against another.**
7. Chafing gear should be placed **at all wearing points of mooring lines.**
8. Chafing gear should be placed at all wearing points of mooring lines, is normally used on mooring lines, reduces and prevents wear caused by the rubbing of one object against another, **all of the above are correct.**

Terms and Definitions

9. One or more sheaves fitted in a wood or metal frame is a **Block.**
10. A smooth, tapered pin, usually of wood, used to open up the strands of a rope for splicing is called a(n) **fid.**
11. A deck fitting, used to secure line or wire rope, consisting of a single body with two protruding horns is called a **cleat.**
12. This statement is TRUE about hooks and shackles, **Shackles are stronger than hooks of the same diameter.**

Watch Keeping

Basic Principles of watchkeeping

Sightings

13. A proper look must be kept **at all times**.
14. A look-out should report objects sighted using **relative bearings**.
15. This is NOT a duty of a look-out **supervise any deck work going on in the area**.
16. A vessel spotted at 45° relative can be reported as **broad on the starboard bow**.

Vessel Maneuvering and Handling

Vessel Handling in Rivers and Estuaries

General

17. An estuary **is a partially enclosed coastal body of brackish water with one or more rivers or streams flowing into it, and with a free connection to the open sea.**
18. River currents tend to **cause the greatest depth of water to be along the outside of a bend**.
19. For the deepest water when rounding the bend in a river, you should navigate your vessel **toward the outside of the bend**.
20. When hugging a bank in a narrow channel, you should take precautions against bank suction, squat and the effects of vessels passing close aboard, clogged sea chests, plugged sea strainers and overheated machinery, striking underwater obstructions close to the bank, **all of the above.**

Maneuvering in Shallow Water

Squat

21. **Squatting** is a shallow water effect that will increase dramatically if you increase your ship's speed past its "critical speed."
22. Your ship is in shallow water and the bow rides up on its bow wave while the stern sinks into a depression of its transverse wave system. This is called **squatting.**
23. Speed through the water has this effect on a vessel which is underway in shallow water, **an increase in speed results in the stern sucking down lower than the bow.**
24. A common occurrence when a vessel is running into shallow water is that **"squat" will cause a decrease in bottom clearance and an increase in draft.**

Interaction with Bank/Passing Ships

Bank Cushion

25. Bank Cushion **forces the bow away from the bank**.
26. Your vessel is proceeding along a narrow channel. The effect called bank cushion **forces the bow away from the bank.**
27. A vessel traveling down a narrow channel may set off the nearer side. This effect is known as **bank cushion**.
28. You are proceeding along a narrow channel and notice your bow is being pushed away from the bank. This is called **bank cushion**.

Bank Suction

29. Your vessel is proceeding along a narrow channel. The effect called bank suction has this effect on the vessel, **it pulls the stern toward the bank.**
30. The effect known as "bank suction" act on a single-screw vessel proceeding along a narrow channel by **pulling the stern toward the bank.**
31. A vessel traveling down a narrow channel may have it's stern pulled into nearer side. This effect is known as **bank suction**.
32. You are proceeding along a narrow channel and notice your stern pulls toward the bank. This is called **bank suction**.

Berthing and Unberthing

Berthing

33. You are mooring to a buoy. You should approach the buoy with the current form **ahead**.
34. The best time to work a boat into a slip is **at slack water**.
35. Your vessel is a single screw ship with a right-hand propeller. There is no current. The easiest way to make a landing is **port side to**.
36. When docking a vessel the most favorable direction of the wind and current are **parallel to the pier from ahead**.

Unberthing

37. After casting off moorings at a mooring buoy in calm weather, you should **back away a few lengths to clear the buoy and then go ahead on the engines**.
38. To warp a vessel means to **move the vessel by hauling on lines**.
39. A twin screw can clear the inboard propeller and maneuver off a pier best by holding a(n) **forward spring line and going slow ahead on the outboard engine**.
40. Your vessel is port side to a pier with a spring line lead aft from the bow. In calm weather, putting the engines ahead with the rudder hard left should bring **the bow in and the stern out**.

Anchoring and Mooring

Scope

41. When anchoring, good practice requires 5 to 7 fathoms of chain for each fathom of depth. In deep water you should use **less chain for each fathom of depth**.
42. When anchoring, it is a common rule of thumb to use a length of chain **five to seven times the depth of water**.
43. Using a scope of five, you should put out **360 feet (110 meters)** to anchor in 12 (72 feet) fathoms of water.
44. Using a scope of 6, use **144 feet** in order to anchor in 24 feet of water.

Bottom

45. Generally speaking, the most favorable bottom for anchoring is **a mixture of mud and clay**.
46. Conventional anchors are least likely to hold in a bottom consisting of **rock**.
47. Of the choices given, the BEST holding ground for conventional anchors is **very soft mud**.
48. The holding capability of an anchor is primarily determined by the **anchor's ability to dig in**.

Heavy Weather Operations

General

49. You are steaming in a heavy gale and find it necessary to heave to. Under most circumstances, it is best done by **taking the seas fine on the bow and reducing the speed to the minimum to hold that position**.
50. When making way in heavy seas you notice your vessel's screw is being lifted clear of the water and racing. One way to correct this would be **decrease speed**.
51. You are underway in heavy weather and your bow is into the seas. To prevent pounding, you should **decrease speed**.
52. When a boat turns broadside to heavy seas and winds, thus exposing the boat to the dangers of capsizing, the boat has **broached**.

Motion

53. When a vessel is swinging from side to side off course due to quartering seas, the vessel is **yawing**.
54. The vertical motion of a floating vessel in which the entire hull is lifted by the force of the sea is known as **heave**.
55. The angular movement of a vessel about a horizontal line drawn from its bow to its stern is **rolling**.
56. Horizontal fore and aft motion of a vessel is known as **surge**.

General: Turning Circle, Pivot Point, Advance and Transfer

Turning Circle

57. This statement about a tunnel bow thruster is TRUE, **It provides lateral control without affecting headway.**
58. The turning circle of a vessel making a turn over 360 degrees is the path followed by the **center of gravity**.
59. The effect of wind on exposed areas of the vessel is most noticeable when **backing**.
60. The distance a vessel moves at right angles to the original course, when a turn of 180° has been completed, is called the **tactical diameter**.

Pivot Point

61. When underway and proceeding ahead, as the speed increases, the pivot point tends to **move forward**.
62. The pivoting point of a vessel going ahead is **about one-third of the vessel's length from the bow**.
63. When backing down with sternway, the pivot point of a vessel is **about one-quarter of the vessel's length from the stern**.
64. When backing the pivot point of the vessel is **about one-quarter of the vessel's length from the stern**.

Advance

65. The distance a vessel moves parallel to the original course from the point where the rudder is put over to any point on the turning circle is called the **advance**.
66. When heading on a course, you put your rudder hard over. The distance traveled parallel to the direction of the original course from where you put your rudder over to any point on the turning circle is known as **advance**.
67. The distance gained in the direction of the original course when you are making a turn is known as **advance**.
68. In relation to the turning circle of a ship, the term "advance" means the distance **gained in the direction of the original course**.

Transfer

69. The distance a vessel moves perpendicular to the original course from the point where the rudder is put over to any point on the turning circle is called the **transfer**.
70. The distance gained at right angles to the original course when you are making a turn is known as **transfer**.
71. In relation to the turning circle of a ship, the term "transfer" means the distance **gained at right angles to the original course**.
72. You are on a course of 000°T and put the rudder right 30°. The direction in which the transfer will be measured is **090°T.**

Wake Reduction

General

73. A stream of water immediately surrounding a moving vessel's hull, flowing in the same direction as the vessel is known as **wake current**.

74. As a ship moves through the water, it drags with it a body of water called the wake. The ratio of the wake speed to the ship's speed is called **wake fraction**.

75. In order to reduce your wake in a narrow channel you should **reduce your speed**.

76. As a ship moves through the water, it causes a wake, which is also moving forward relative to the sea. In addition to a fore and aft motion, this wake also has a(n) **upward and inward flow**.

Vessel Power Plant

Small Engine Operation and Maintenance

Propeller

77. The force exerted by a propeller which tends to throw the stern right or left is called **sidewise force (prop walk)**.

78. The distance that a ship moves forward with each revolution of its propeller, if there is no slip, is called **pitch**.

79. The forward movement of a vessel in one revolution of its propeller is measured by **the pitch**.

80. The pitch of a propeller is a measure of the **number of feet per revolution the propeller is designed to advance in still water without slip**.

Single Screw

81. When a vessel with a single right-hand propeller back to port the **bow falls off to starboard**.

82. You are on a single-screw vessel with a right-handed propeller. The vessel is going full speed astern with full right rudder. The bow will swing **probably to port**.

83. You are aboard a single-screw vessel with a right-handed propeller. The vessel is dead in the water and the rudder is amidships. If you reverse your engines you would expect your vessel to **kick its stern to port**.

84. In order to back a right-handed, single-screw vessel in a straight line, you will probably need to use **some right rudder**.

Twin Screw

85. While moving ahead, a twin-screw ship has an advantage over a single-screw ship because **side forces will be eliminated**.
86. A twin-screw ship going ahead on the starboard screw only tends to move **to port**.
87. A twin-screw ship going ahead on the port screw only tends to move **to starboard**.
88. The BEST way to steer a twin-screw vessel if you lose your rudder is by using **one engine running at reduced speed and controlling the vessel with the other**.

Maritime Law

National Maritime Law

Certification and Documentation of Vessels

89. This type of life preserver must be carried for each person on board an uninspected passenger vessel, **type I.**
90. A vessel must have one approved ring life buoy on board if its length is over **26 feet.**
91. The document which shows a vessel's nationality, ownership, and tonnage is the **Certificate of Documentation**.
92. This US agency assigns an official number to a vessel, **Coast Guard.**

Rules and Regulations for Uninspected Vessels

93. Failure to comply with, or enforce, the provisions of the "Vessel Bridge-to-Bridge Radiotelephone Act" can result in a **$650 civil penalty charged against the person in charge of the vessel**.
94. You are in charge of a U.S. documented vessel. Under title 46 of the United States Code, if you fail to report a complaint of a sexual offense, you may be **civilly charged and fined**.
95. Under federal regulations, the minimum level of Blood Alcohol Content (BAC) that constitutes a violation of the laws prohibiting Boating Under the Influence of Alcohol (BUI) on commercial vessels is **0.04% (BAC)**.
96. By law, a user of marijuana shall be subject to **revocation of license or certificate**.

Pollution Prevention Regulations

97. Pollution of the waterways may result from the discharge of sewage, the galley trash can, an oily mixture of one part per million, **all of the above**.
98. This type of pollution is prohibited from being discharged anywhere in the world, at any time, **plastic.**
99. You detect oil around your tank vessel while discharging. The FIRST thing to do is **shut down operations**.

100. When oil is accidentally discharged into the water, you should **contain the oil and remove as much of it as possible from the water** after reporting the discharge.

Credentialing of Seaman

101. Operator of Uninspected Passenger Vessels are required to keeps their Coast Guard License aboard **only when carrying passengers for hire**.
102. Total responsibility for shipping and discharging the seaman is that of the **Master of the vessel**.
103. **The Master of the vessel** is responsible for properly manning a vessel in accordance with all applicable laws, regulations and international conventions.
104. This document shows the minimum required crew a vessel must have to navigate from one port in the United States to another, **Certificate of Inspection.**

Shipboard Management and Training

Ship Sanitation

105. Potable water is **water that is safe to drink or to use for food preparation**.
106. Any portion of the potable water system which has been contaminated should be **cleaned, disinfected, and flushed before the affected units are placed in operation**.
107. Keeping down or eliminating the rodent population on a vessel may involve the use of **poisons and traps**.
108. A "Marine Sanitation Device" or MSD is another way to describe a vessel's **toilet**.

Safety

109. Your vessel has gone aground in waters where the tide is falling. The BEST action you can take is to **set out a kedge anchor**.
110. These safety checks should be made before letting go the anchor; see that the anchor is clear of obstructions, see that the chain is all clear, see that the wildcat is disengaged, **all of the above.**
111. Your vessel is broken down and rolling in heavy seas. You can reduce danger of capsizing by **rigging a sea anchor**.
112. Flammable liquids should have a **red** label.

Ships Business

Certificates and Signals

Certificates

113. The Tonnage Certificate indicates **net tons**.
114. If your vessel is equipped with a radiotelephone, you must also have a **radio station license** aboard.
115. A vessel's Certificate of Documentation **must be carried on board**.
116. Official proof of an American vessel's nationality is contained in the **Certificate of Documentation**.

Signals

117. The service life of distress signals must be not more than **forty two months from the date of manufacture**.
118. For the purposes of distress signaling, small passenger vessels that operate on runs of more than 30 minutes duration on lakes, bays and sounds, and river routes must carry **three hand red flare distress signals, and three hand orange smoke distress signals**.
119. Distress flares and smoke signals for small passenger vessels are not required aboard vessels on runs of less than 30 minutes duration, must be Coast Guard approved and stowed in a portable, watertight container, must be marked with an expiration date not more than 42 months from the date of manufacture, **all of the above**.
120. These small passenger vessels are NOT required to carry a Category 1 406 MHz EPIRB; a coastwise vessel whose route does not take it more than three miles from shore, a vessel operating on lakes, bays, sounds, and rivers, a vessel operating within three miles from the coastline of the Great Lakes, **all of the above**.

Fire Prevention and Firefighting Appliances

Basic Firefighting and Prevention

Prevention

121. Small quantities of flammable liquids needed at a work site should be **in a metal container with a tight cap**.
122. Spontaneous ignition can result from **careless disposal or storage of material**.
123. A chemical additive to LPG (Liquid Propane Gas) gives it a characteristic **odor**.
124. Storage batteries should be charged in a well ventilated area because **they emit hydrogen**.

Spread

125. The spread of fire is prevented by **removing combustibles from the endangered area**.
126. To prevent the spread of fire by convection you should **close all openings to the area**.
127. You are underway when a fire breaks out in the forward part of your vessel. If possible, you should **put the vessel's stern into the wind**.
128. A fire in the galley ALWAYS poses the additional threat of **a grease fire in the ventilation system**.

Electrical

129. You are fighting a fire in the electrical switchboard in the engine room. You should secure the power, then **use a portable CO2 extinguisher**.
130. **Danger of shock to personnel** is the MOST important consideration when determining how to fight an electrical fire.
131. An important step in fighting any electrical fire is to **de-energize the circuit**.
132. When electrical equipment is involved in a fire, the stream of dry chemicals should be **aimed at the source of the flame**.

Classes of Fire

A, B, C, D, K

133. Class A fire is in **paper , wood, cloth, trash and other common materials**.
134. Class B fire is in **gasoline, oil, paint and other flammable liquids**.
135. Class C fire is in **live electrical equipment**.
136. Class D fire is in **metal and metal alloys**.
137. Class K fire is in **cooking media, vegetable oil, animal fats and oils**.

Chemistry of Fire

Fire Triangle

138. The Fire Triangle is **a diagram for understanding the necessary ingredients for most fires**.
139. A diagram for understanding the necessary ingredients for most fires is the **fire triangle**.
140. All of the following are part of the fire triangle EXCEPT **electricity**.
141. Fire triangle is composed of fuel, heat, oxygen, **all of the above**.

Emergency Procedures

Passenger/Crew Safety in Emergencies

Communication

142. The VHF radiotelephone calling/safety/distress frequency is **156.8 MHz (channel 16)**.
143. A vessel in distress should send by radiotelephone the two-tone alarm signal followed immediately by the **spoken words "Mayday, Mayday, Mayday"**.
144. You are using VHF channel 16 (156.8 MHz) or 2182 kHz. You need help but are not in danger. You should use the urgent signal **"PAN-PAN"**.
145. The **SECURITE** safety signal call word is spoken three times, followed by the station call letters spoken three times, to announce a storm warning, danger to navigation, or special aid to navigation.

Drills

146. **Recovering an individual from the water** emergency is required to be covered at the required periodic drills on a fishing vessel.
147. Coast Guard regulations require that all of the following emergencies be covered at the periodic drills on a fishing vessel EXCEPT **emergency towing**.
148. A new crew member aboard your fishing vessel, who has not received any safety instructions or participated in any drills, reports on board. The Master must provide a safety orientation **before sailing**.
149. While reading the muster list you see that "3 short blasts on the whistle and 3 short rings of the bell" is the signal for **dismissal from fire and emergency stations**.

Man Overboard Procedures

General

150. A Man Overboard situation is one in which **someone has fallen overboard**.
151. The key to rescuing a man overboard is **well-conducted drills**.
152. A person who sees someone fall overboard should **call for help and keep the individual in sight**.
153. On a small boat, if someone fell overboard and you did not know over which side the person fell, you should **stop the propellers from turning and throw a ring buoy over the side**.

Watch

154. You are standing the wheel watch when you hear the cry, "Man overboard starboard side". You should instinctively **give full right rudder**.
155. A crew member has just fallen overboard off your port side. You should **immediately put the rudder over hard left**.
156. You receive word that a person has fallen overboard from the starboard side. You should FIRST **put the wheel hard right**.
157. A person has fallen overboard and is being picked up with a lifeboat. If the person appears in danger of drowning, the lifeboat should make **the most direct approach**.

Turns

158. The Williamson turn is **suitable for both immediate and delayed action situations**.
159. The Scharnow turn is **not appropriate in an immediate action situation**.
160. The Racetrack turn is **also called the two turn approach**.
161. The single turn is **useful on small vessels is immediate situations**.

Abandon Ship Procedures

General

162. If passengers are on board when an abandon ship drill is carried out, they should **take part**.
163. If, for any reason, it is necessary to abandon ship while far out at sea, it is important that the crew members should **remain together in the area because rescuers will start searching at the vessel's last known position**.
164. After abandoning ship everyone should **remain together in the vessel's last known position**.
165. If you reach shore in a life raft, the first thing to do is **drag the raft ashore and lash it down for a shelter**.

Abandon Ship Training and Drills

166. Material for abandon-ship training must be **aboard each vessel**.
167. Material for abandon-ship training must contain instructions and information about the lifesaving appliances aboard the vessel and about **the best methods of survival**.
168. Any crew member excused from an abandon-ship drill must participate in the next one, so that each member participates in at least one each **month**.
169. As far as practicable, each abandon-ship drill must be conducted as if there were **an actual emergency**.

Collision

Damage Control

170. A vessel is described as a two compartment vessel when it **will float if any two adjacent compartments are flooded**.
171. A vessel of not more than 65 feet in length must have a collision bulkhead if it carries more than **49 passengers**.
172. In plugging submerged holes; rags, wedges, and other materials should be used in conjunction with plugs to **reduce the water leaking around the plugs**.
173. When plugging holes below the waterline you should **reduce the entry of water as much as possible**.

Temporary Repairs

General

174. A crack in the deck plating of a vessel may be temporarily prevented from increasing in length by **drilling a hole at each end of the crack**.
175. The objective of shoring a damaged bulkhead is to **support and hold the damaged area in the damaged position**.
176. Hull **damage at or just above the waterline** should be repaired first.
177. Repairing damage to the hull at or above the waterline reduces the threat of **continued progressive downflooding**.

Fire Explosion

General

178. You should be most concerned about a possible explosion or fire in fuel tanks **during fueling when fuel first strikes the tank bottom**.
179. You hear the general alarm and ships whistle sound for over 10 seconds. Traditionally, this is the signal for **fire and emergency**.

180. You are underway when a fire breaks out in the forward part of your vessel. If possible you should **put the vessel's stern into the wind**.

181. There is a fire aft aboard your vessel. To help fight the fire, you should **head the bow into the wind and decrease speed**.

Emergency Towing

General

182. A tug is approaching a broken down vessel to take it in tow in moderately heavy weather. In most cases the **tug should approach from downwind**.

183. A vessel brought alongside should be fended off the towing vessel by **fenders**.

184. The biggest problem you generally encounter when towing a single tow astern **yaw**.

185. The greatest danger of an overriding tow is **collision between the tow and the stern of the towing vessel.**

Lifesaving

Survival at Sea

CPR

General

186. CPR is **an emergency procedure that combines chest compressions often with artificial ventilation in an effort to manually preserve intact brain function until further measures are taken to restore spontaneous blood circulation and breathing in a person who is in cardiac arrest.**

187. When starting CPR on a drowning victim, you should **begin mouth-to-mouth ventilations as soon as possible**.

188. The MOST important element in administering CPR is **starting the treatment quickly**.

189. Before CPR is started, you should **establish an open airway**.

First Aid

Bleeding

190. In all but the most severe cases, bleeding from a wound should be controlled by **applying direct pressure to the wound**.

191. The preferred method of controlling external bleeding is by **direct pressure on the wound**.

192. A person has suffered a laceration of the arm. Severe bleeding has been controlled by using a sterile dressing and direct pressure. Next you should **apply a pressure**

bandage over the dressing.
193.   A tourniquet should be used to control bleeding ONLY **when all other means have failed**.

Breaks

194.   A person suffering from possible broken bones and internal injuries should **not be moved but made comfortable until medical assistance arrives**.
195.   You should FIRST treat a simple fracture by **preventing further movement of the bone**.
196.   A compound fracture is a fracture in which **the bone may be visible**.
197.   The most serious type of fracture is **compound.**

Life Saving Appliance Operations for T-Boats

Life Jacket

198.   PFD stands for **Personal Flotation Device**
199.   This statement is TRUE concerning life preservers (Type I personal flotation devices); **life preservers are designed to turn an unconscious person's face clear of the water.**
200.   Kapok life jackets should NOT be stowed near open flame or where smoking is permitted, used as seats, pillows, or foot rests, left on open decks, **all of the above.**
201.   This statement is TRUE concerning life jackets which are severely damaged, **they should be replaced.**